Colour Pencils

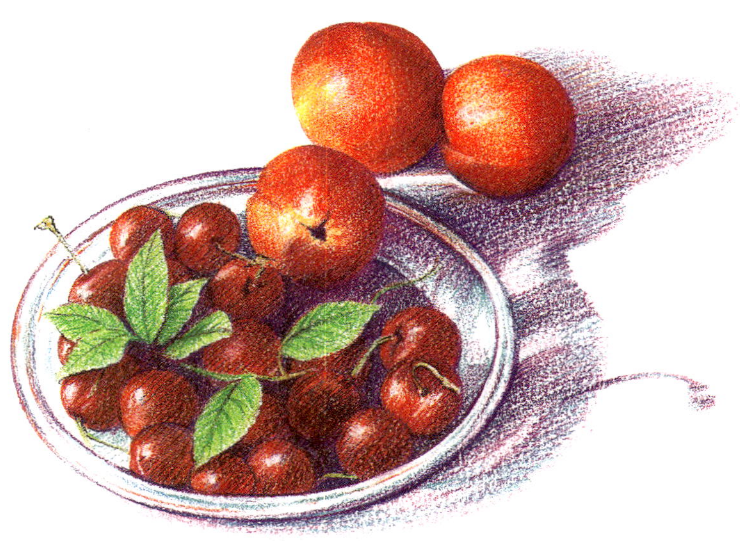

WORKSTATION *is a new concept comprising all the elements you need to commence the art of colour pencils. The first 48 pages offer a comprehensively illustrated introduction to this rewarding pastime. Included at the back of this book are 16 pages of good quality cartridge paper to enable you to use your colour pencils.*

ROD HOLT

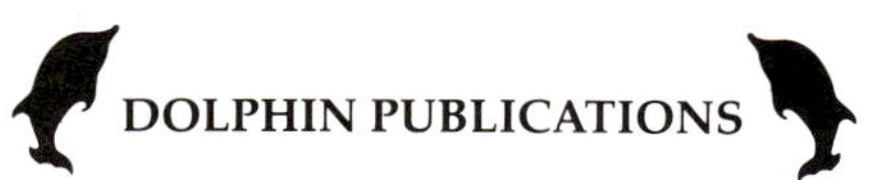

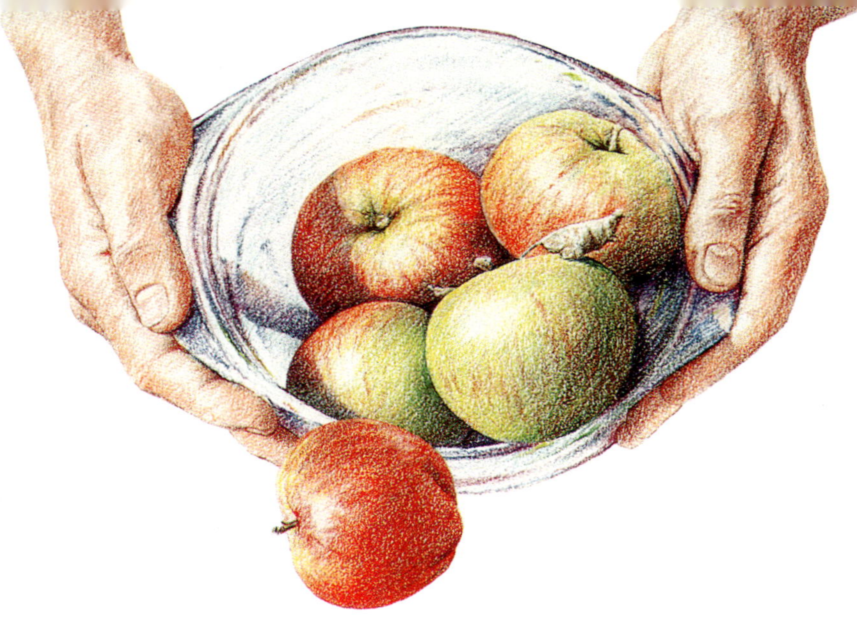

This edition specially produced in 1993 for Dolphin Publications,
Bridge Mills Business Park, Langley Road South, Pendleton, Salford M6 6EL,
by Design Eye Publishing Limited, 8 Fouberts Place, London W1V 1HH.

ISBN 1 872700 14 4

We would like to thank Intercare Products Ltd for the use of the
Tixylix illustration on page 42

Manufactured in China by Giftech Ltd.

A DESIGN EYE BOOK

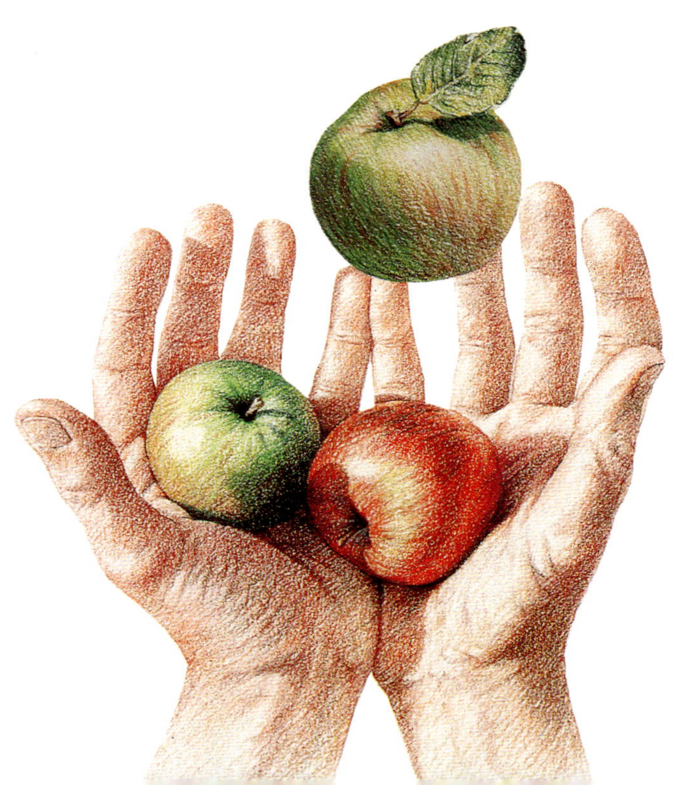

CONTENTS

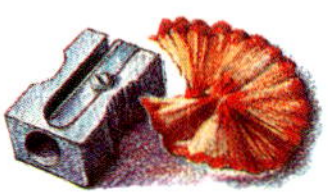

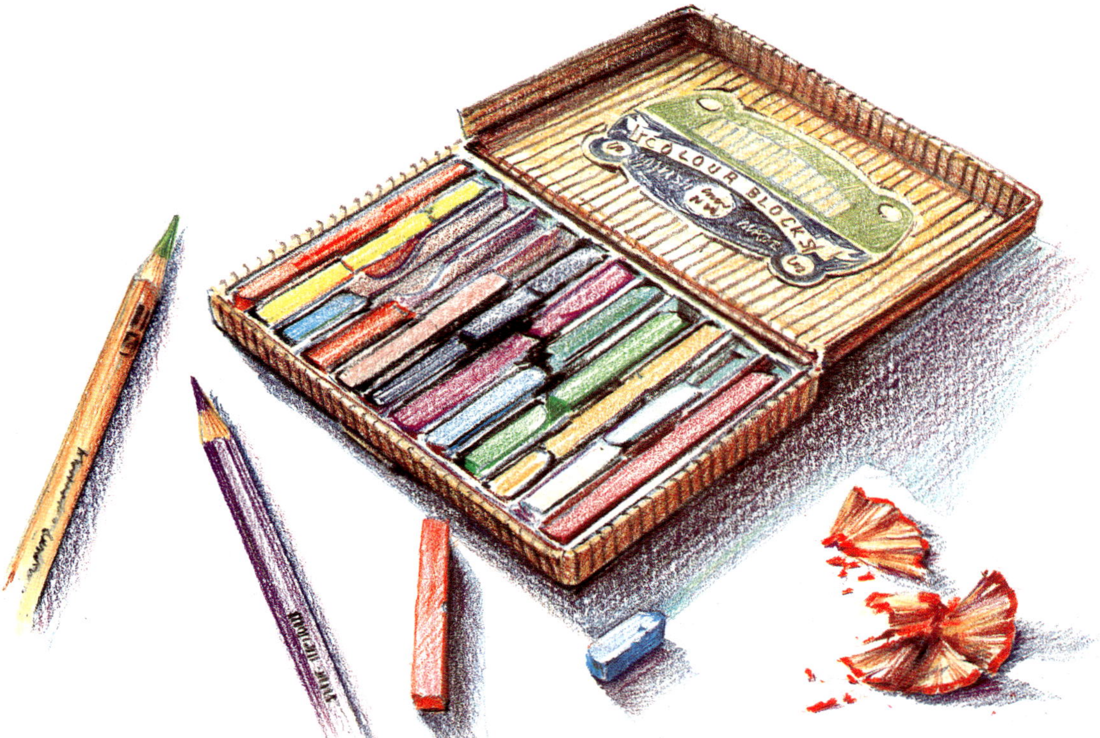

INTRODUCTION

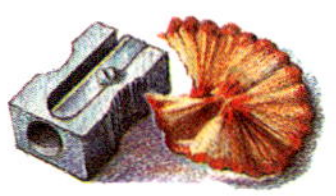

Coloured pencils are, in many ways, the easiest and cheapest medium with which to produce pictures. All you need is a range of colours and paper or a sketch pad; it's both clean and convenient. With a little of the appropriate knowledge and some practice, it is possible to produce images of great visual richness.

During the course of this book, we shall discover the many different types of coloured pencil available, their various qualities, and the different ways in which each can be used. Armed with this information, it will then be up to you to choose whichever suits you best.

It is true to say that there is no 'one' correct way to use coloured pencils. Only by experimenting will you discover the true depth of this medium and thus enjoy it to its full.

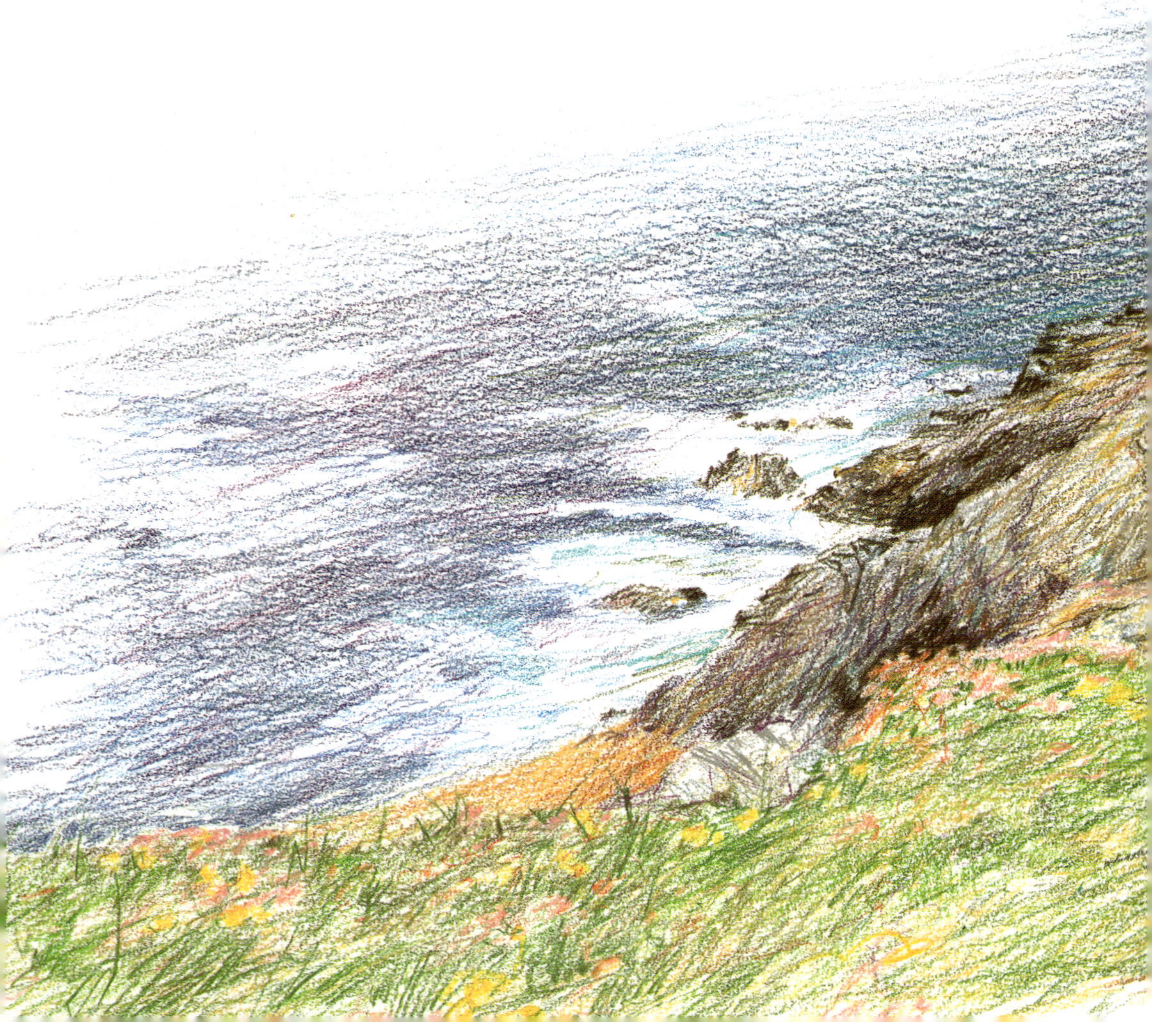

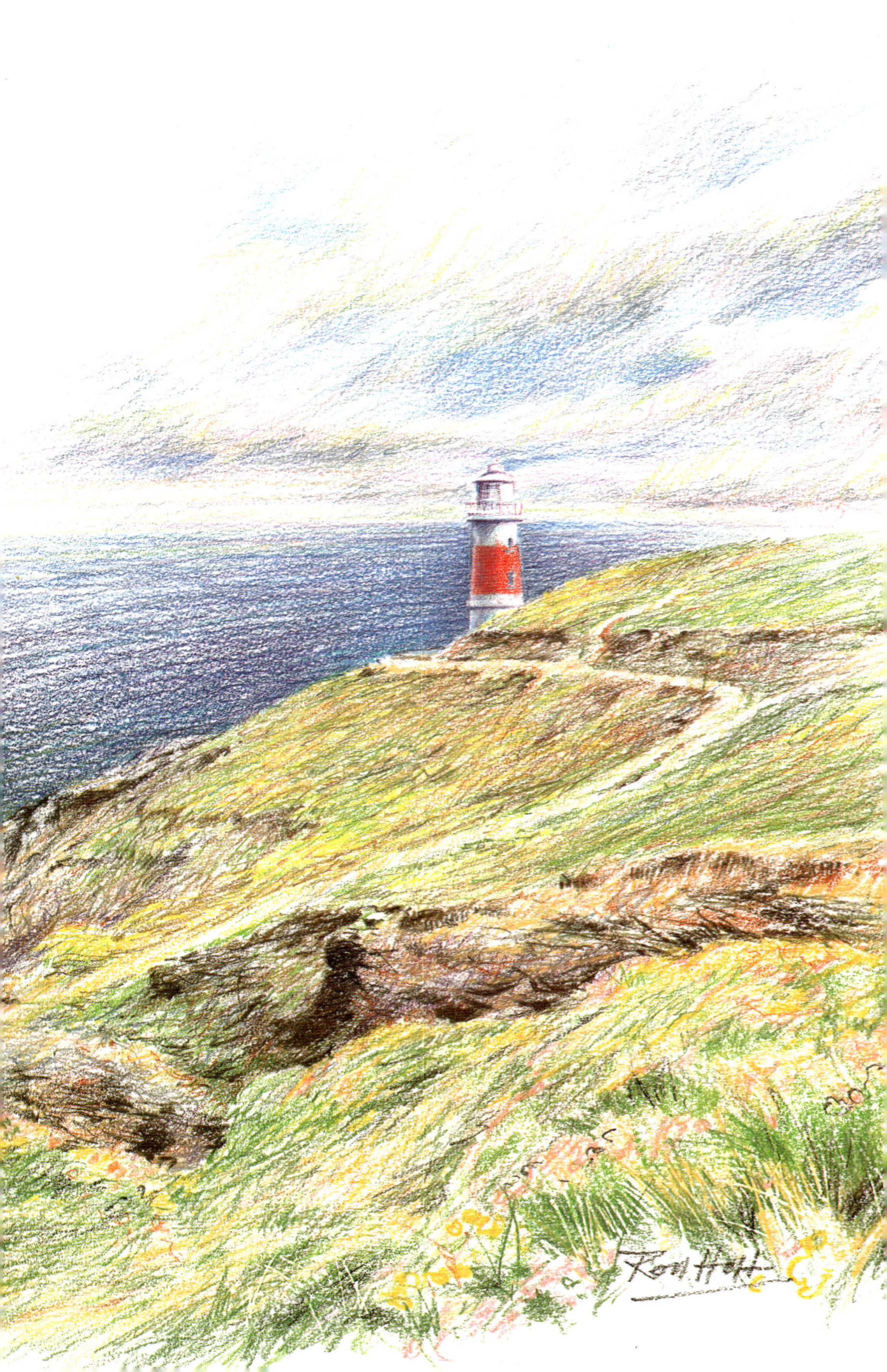

EQUIPMENT

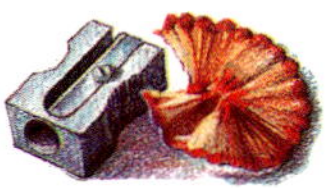

AT THE BACK OF THE BOOK, you will find the basic materials required for making drawings. There is obviously a vast variety you can acquire as you become more accomplished. To some degree, however, I feel that the best results are produced using the simplest materials.

It is, after all, what you give to the medium that brings it to life. This is the essential joy of colour pencil work: simplicity is all – no messy peripheral equipment, just pencils, paper and you.

As you progress you will acquire a great variety of pencils. A good strong box or tin to store them in is very useful.

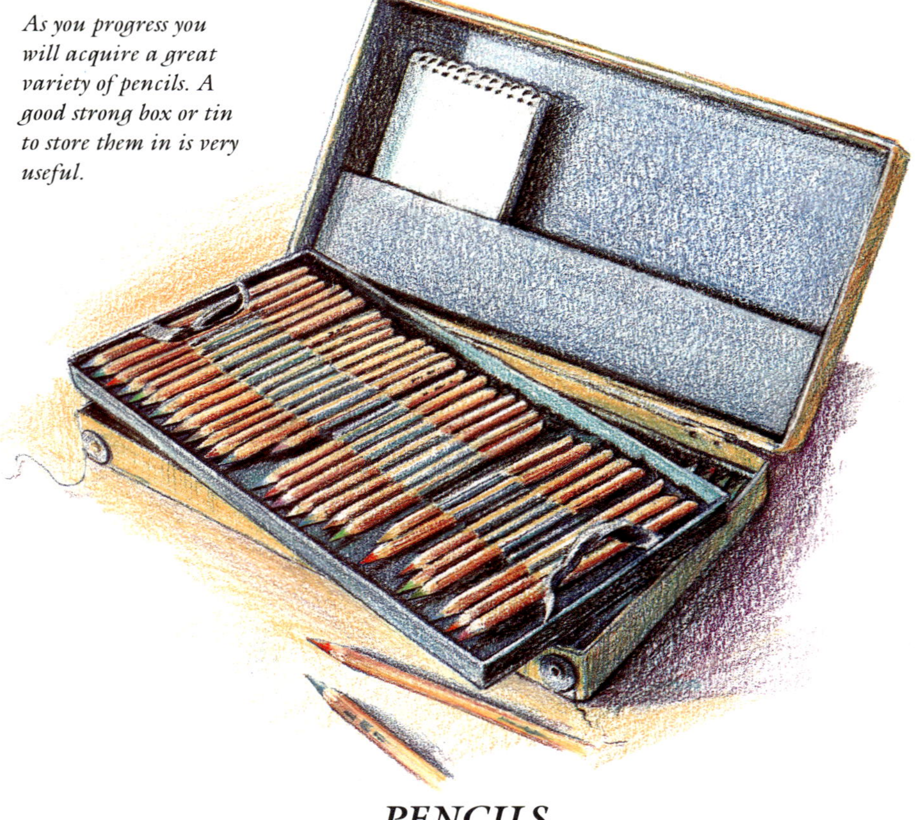

PENCILS

It is well worth trying the many different types of pencil now available to the artist working in coloured pencils. The main types are:
• ***wax pencils***, which vary from hard to soft and are without doubt the most commonly used

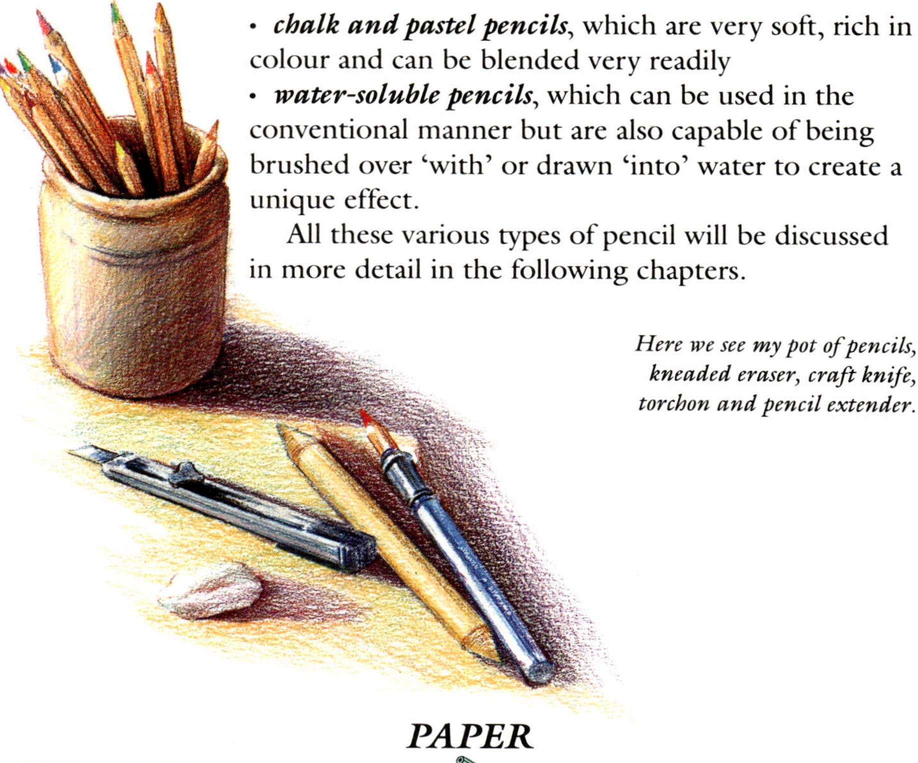

• *chalk and pastel pencils*, which are very soft, rich in colour and can be blended very readily
• *water-soluble pencils*, which can be used in the conventional manner but are also capable of being brushed over 'with' or drawn 'into' water to create a unique effect.

All these various types of pencil will be discussed in more detail in the following chapters.

Here we see my pot of pencils, kneaded eraser, craft knife, torchon and pencil extender.

PAPER

The paper on which you work can have a very significant effect on the end results. The different types of paper include:
• *textured cartridge paper*, which will break up the colour and marks you make, giving a diffuse quality to the image
• *a smooth paper*, which will allow each mark you make to be unbroken and clear
• *coloured paper*, which can be useful to create certain effects

Other equipment
You will also need:
• a pencil sharpener or craft knife
• a plastic eraser for making corrections
• a kneaded eraser to lift excess colour from the surface of the paper.

Another useful, but not essential, piece of equipment is a 'torchon', which is a roll of very tightly wound paper in the shape of a pencil, used for blending colours. As we progress through the chapters, other specific pieces of equipment will be mentioned from time to time, but we now have all we need to get started.

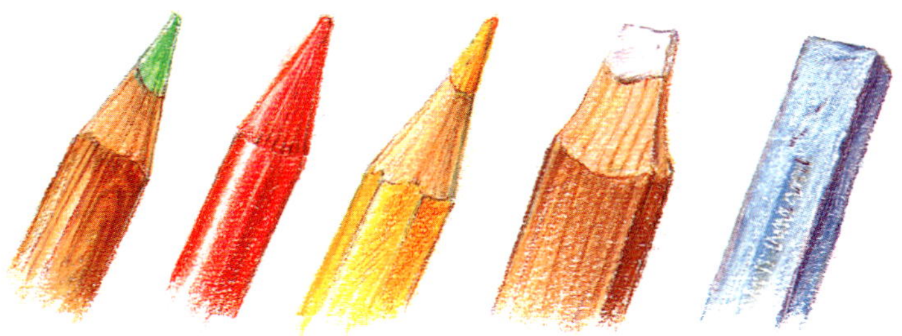

TECHNIQUES

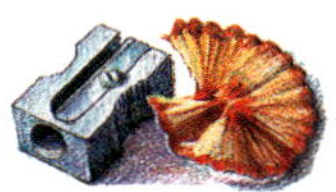

Lthough coloured pencils are, in themselves, a simple medium to use, there are many techniques you will need to learn to get the best from your pencils. Do not be afraid to experiment, as this is by far the best way to learn what they are capable of. You will also find drawing much more fun and more challenging if you allow yourself to be open to new ideas.

As a result, this enjoyment and energy will filter throughout into your pictures, giving them both vitality and strength. I cannot overstress the importance of 'enjoying' your medium to the full. If there is a single quality that will bring your drawings to life, this is it.

Conversely, if you are bored or frustrated, this will kill a drawing stone dead. Something to be avoided at all costs!

Over the next few pages, we will discuss a whole range of techniques that will help you make drawings containing variety and style. One of the keys to producing vibrant, expressive images is the extent to which the artist is able to use the full range of his medium to convey the 'feeling' and 'sensation' of the subject matter.

If you are drawing a composition of soft velvety peaches, then it is appropriate to use soft velvety marks to portray them. If they are on a hard shiny surface, then you must strive to find the most expressive means of conveying the hardness and shine of that surface. Look first, and then trust your own judgement.

To achieve such results will require diligent practice and experimentation of the following techniques. We will begin by discussing the various kinds of marks that coloured pencils can make.

HATCHING

This describes the process of laying a series of parallel strokes of varying lengths on to the drawing. By altering the space between the marks, the

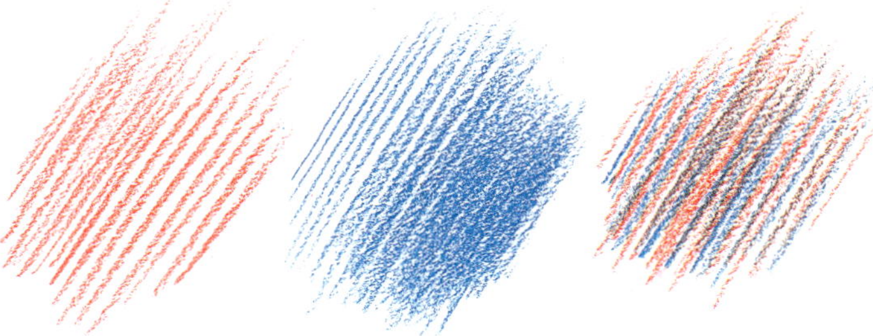

These examples show the effects of hatching with open marks compared with tightly knit hatches and lines of more than one colour running together.

intensity of the colour and tone is adjusted, allowing more or less of the paper surface to show through. By combining various colours together, a rich optical mix can be achieved.

CROSS HATCHING

This is when a series of hatches is overlaid by another series of hatches at a different angle, thus forming a more intricate optical mix than that of hatching alone. Once again, by using a variety of colours, tremendously rich visual effects can be obtained.

Cross hatching can be done using more than one colour to produce various effects.

In this drawing we see an example of hatching in which most of the pencil marks are made in the same direction. This gives the drawing an overall unity, the colours blending smoothly together.

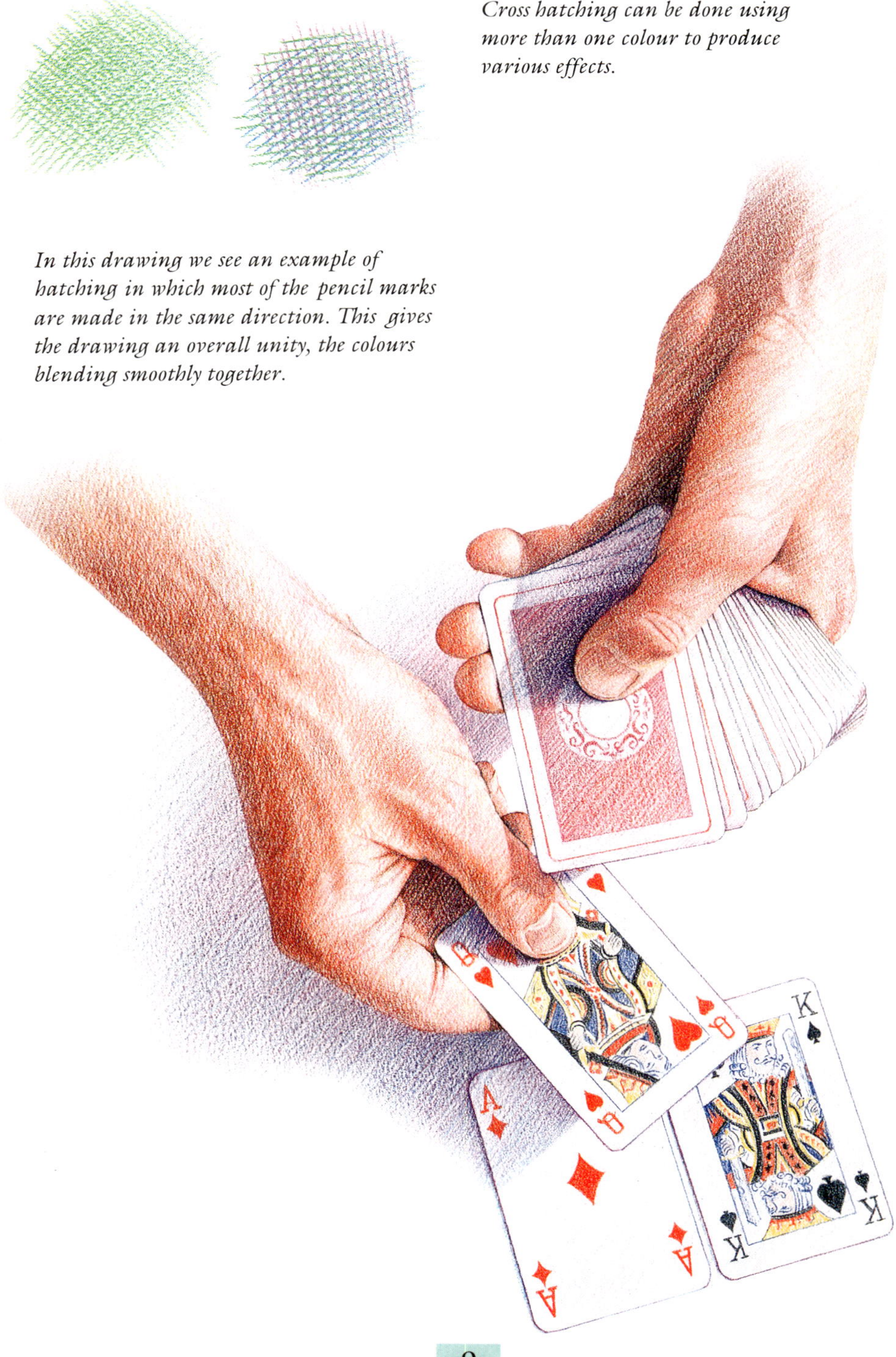

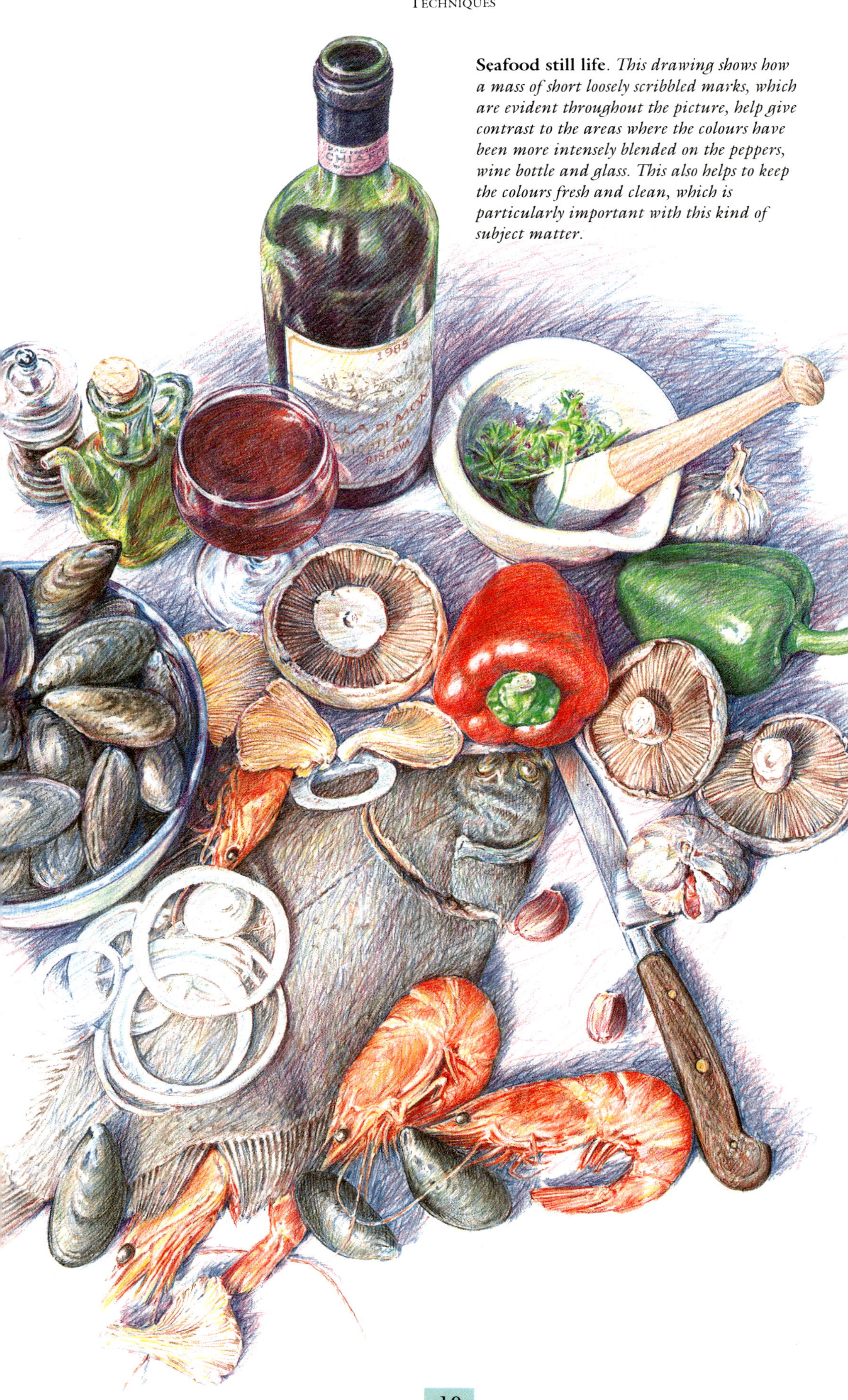

Seafood still life. *This drawing shows how a mass of short loosely scribbled marks, which are evident throughout the picture, help give contrast to the areas where the colours have been more intensely blended on the peppers, wine bottle and glass. This also helps to keep the colours fresh and clean, which is particularly important with this kind of subject matter.*

BLENDING

This is the result of two or more different colours mixing together to make a new colour. A smooth, gradual change of colour and tone is achieved by overlaying a series of closely hatched marks of varying intensity. Soft velvety pencils lend themselves particularly to smooth blending.

Care should be taken with the choice of colours as the wrong colours blended together can become dull and muddy. If you are in any doubt about any combination of colours, it is wise to test it out first on a rough piece of paper before committing yourself.

Creating a more textural blend can be achieved by using more 'active' marks, as with more open hatching and cross hatching. Scribbled 'squiggles' can also be used as an effective optical blend. They are very useful, too, for describing form. Dots, dashes and ticks can also be combined to varying degrees.

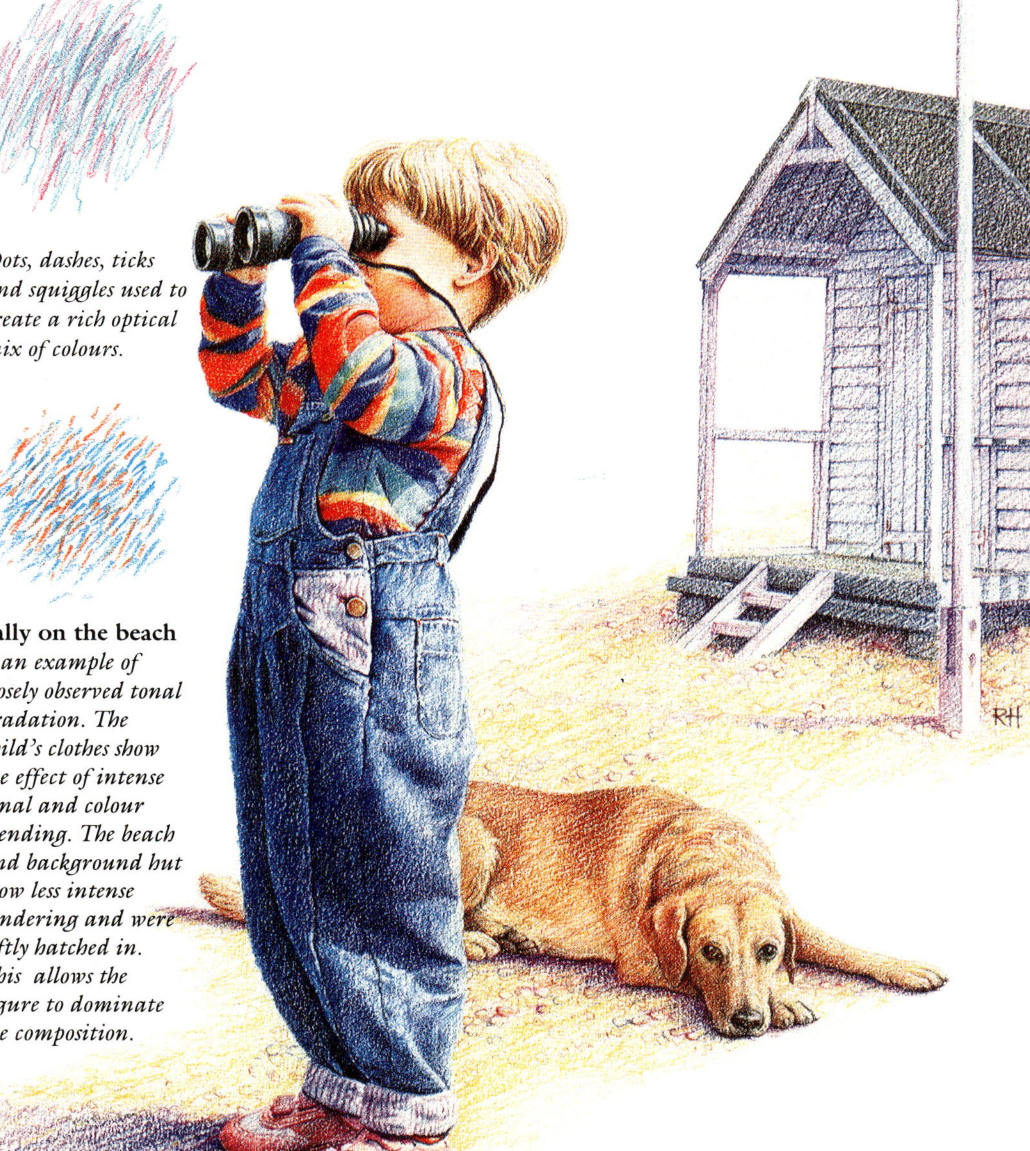

Dots, dashes, ticks and squiggles used to create a rich optical mix of colours.

Sally on the beach *is an example of closely observed tonal gradation. The child's clothes show the effect of intense tonal and colour blending. The beach and background hut show less intense rendering and were softly hatched in. This allows the figure to dominate the composition.*

BURNISHING

This is a technique that takes blending a step further. The process involves applying a layer of light colour, most commonly white over a darker existing colour, thus blending the two together and heightening the surface impact. Burnishing creates a smooth waxy finish, the grain of the paper becoming saturated with colour. It is an effective technique, but one that must be used with care, as a drawing can soon look muddy if the whole surface is burnished. Once again, practice will help you decide when its use is appropriate.

White is the most commonly used burnishing colour, but it is possible to use any colour that is lighter than the colour to be burnished. The following examples show the effect of several different top colours applied over the same base colour.

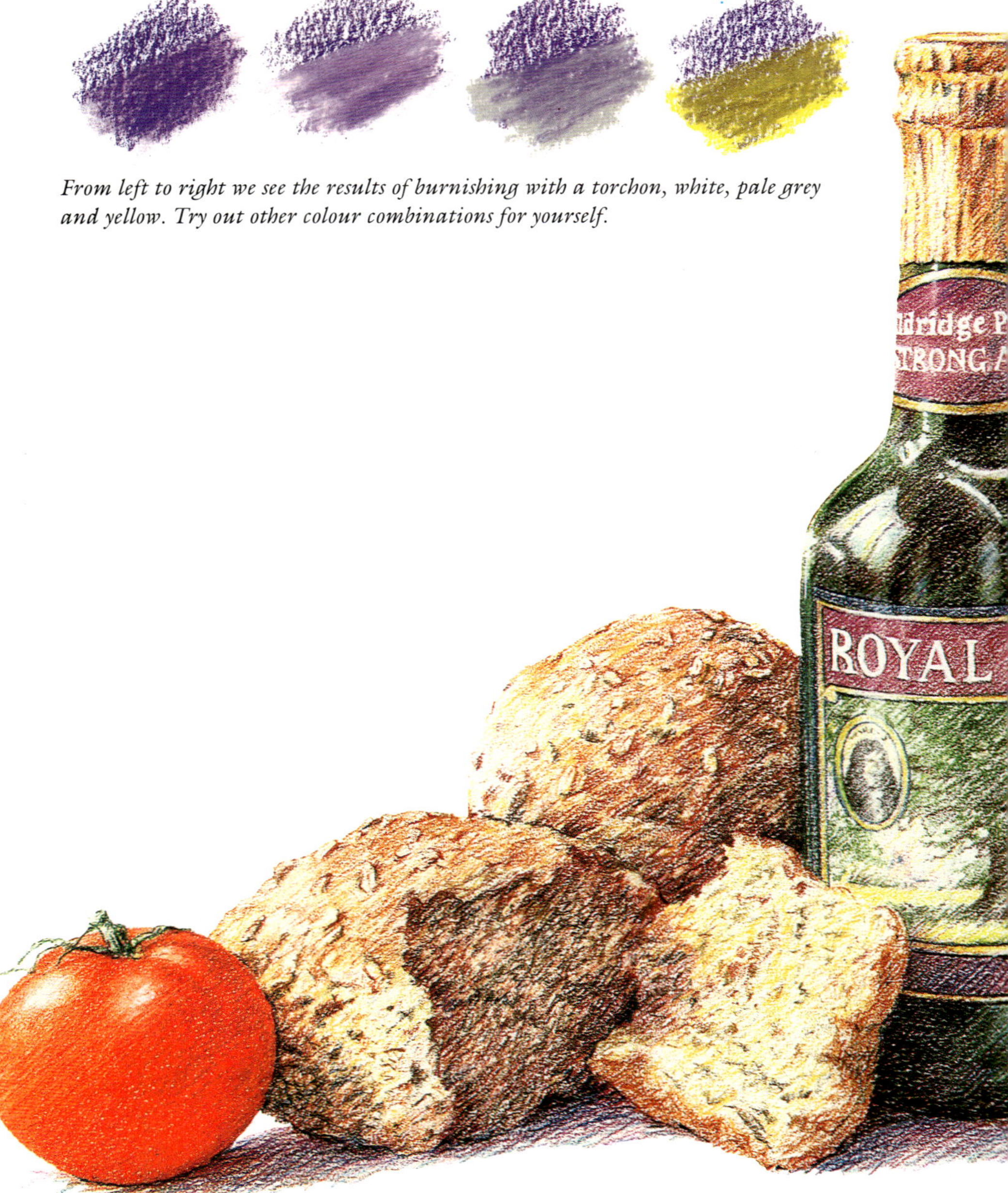

From left to right we see the results of burnishing with a torchon, white, pale grey and yellow. Try out other colour combinations for yourself.

SGRAFFITO

This is a technique using the sharp point of a blade to scratch off colour
and so reveal the various layers of colour laid underneath. Used
correctly, it is very useful for putting the highlights into a drawing and
thus bringing it to life (we will discuss highlights later in the book). It is
a particularly effective technique in areas where there are several layers of
richly built-up colours, the top layer being strong and dark, thus
creating the maximum contract.

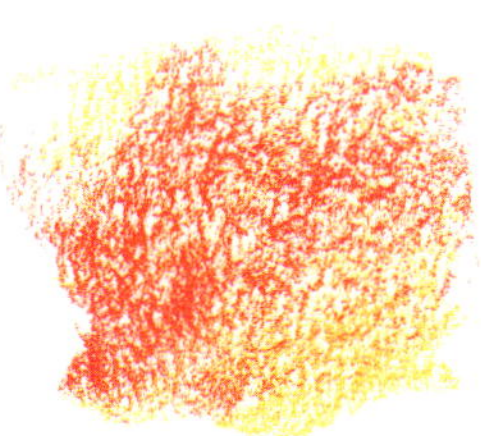  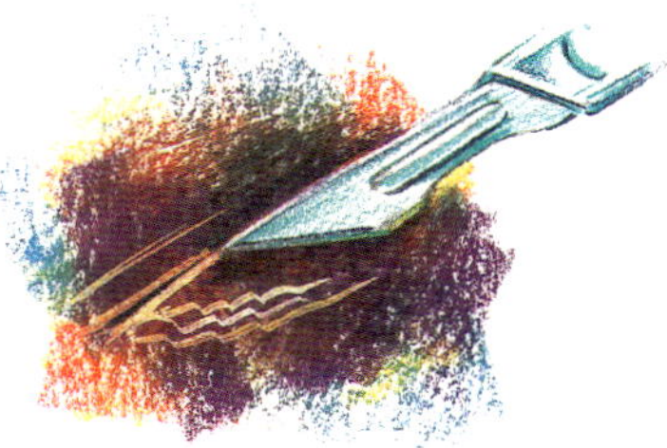

*You can see that by not scratching right down to the paper surface, the various layers of
colour are exposed in a quite unique way. It is possible to make a complete drawing using
this method, which is similar in its way to scraperboard. This is done by layering several
colours in sequence from light to dark and using the point to scratch out a negative image.*

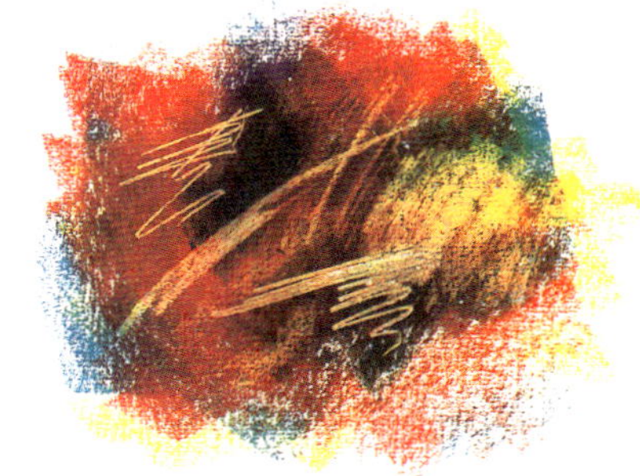

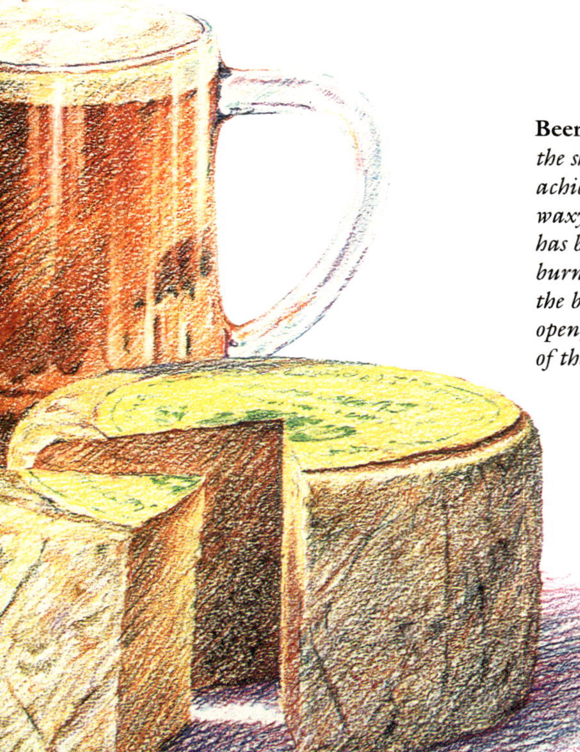

Beer and Cheese still life. *In this picture,
the shine on the bottle and glass has been
achieved by burnishing the surface. Also, the
waxy translucent quality of the tomato skin
has been heightened using a closely shaded
burnish of white. In contrast, the dry feel of
the bread and cheese is achieved using more
open, expressive marks which allow the grain
of the paper to show through.*

IMPRESSED LINE

This is another method that produces a negative line. As the name implies, the marks or lines are actually pressed into the surface of the paper by covering the drawing with a sheet of tracing paper and then drawing through this with a pointed implement (a hard but not too sharp pencil is ideal), so that an invisible series of marks is left on the paper. When you draw gently over this area, the indented lines will remain white, as long as the pencil is allowed to glide over them rather than draw right into them.

This is a useful technique for laying down outlines, and also for making light thin lines – say, thin strands of grass or hair, for example – which can be almost impossible to create in any other way.

If a colour tint is put over the paper before a line is impressed, the indentation will actually retain that colour. This is known as colour· impressing.

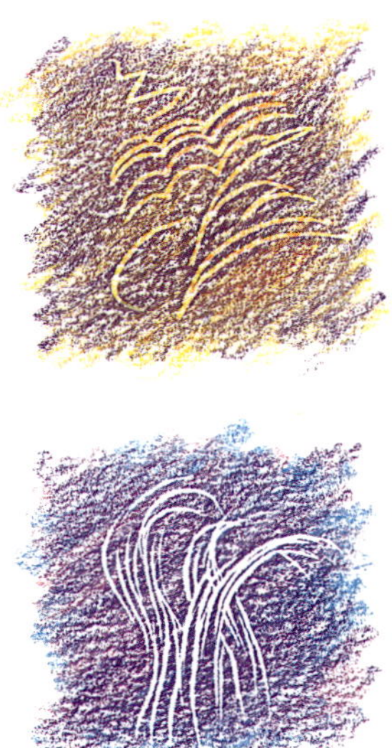

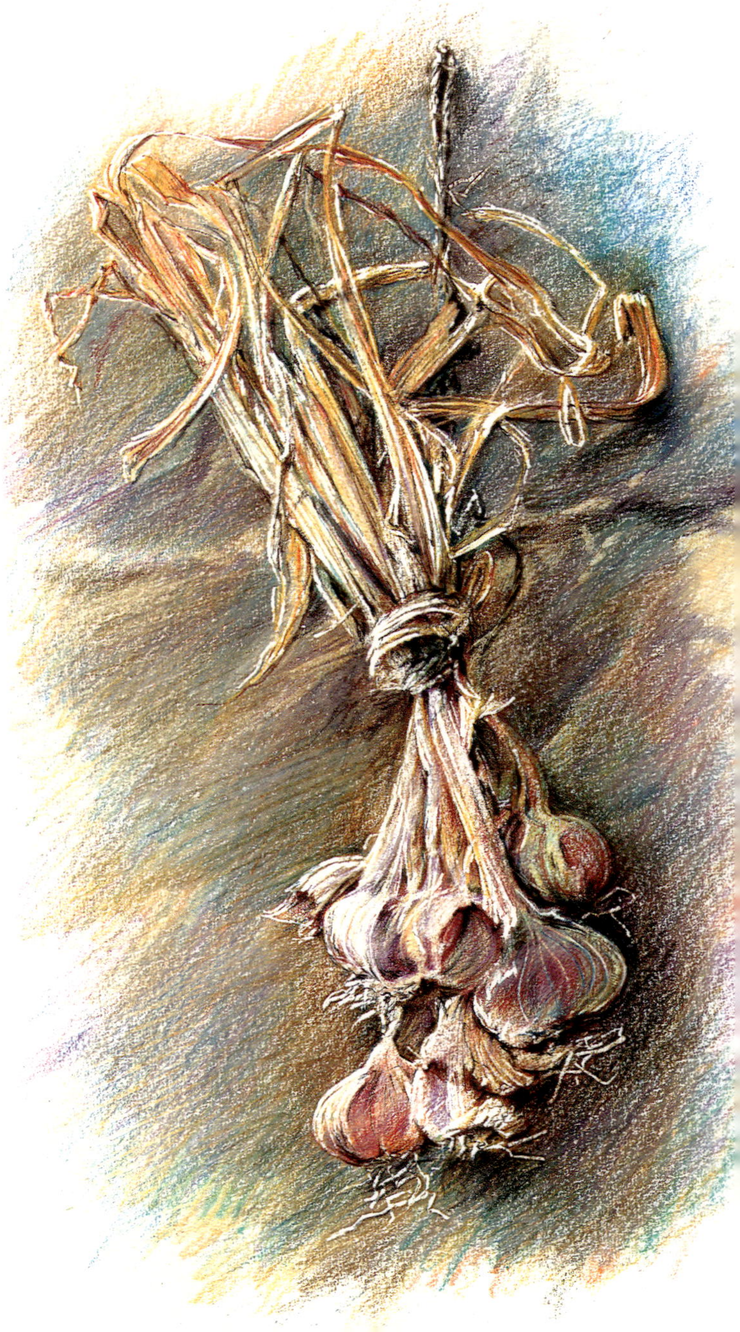

We can see here how the lines depicting the dry leaves and roots of the garlic have been impressed into the paper surface prior to applying colour.

FROTTAGE

This employs a technique similar to that used when making brass rubbings. A textured surface is placed under the drawing and its impression then comes through when shaded over. As a technique, it is commonly used in an abstract manner but it can be very useful for creating areas of high detail in more conventional drawings. The examples given here show the effect of some of the textures most frequently used.

Here are some common examples of frottage: pottery, wood grain and stone.

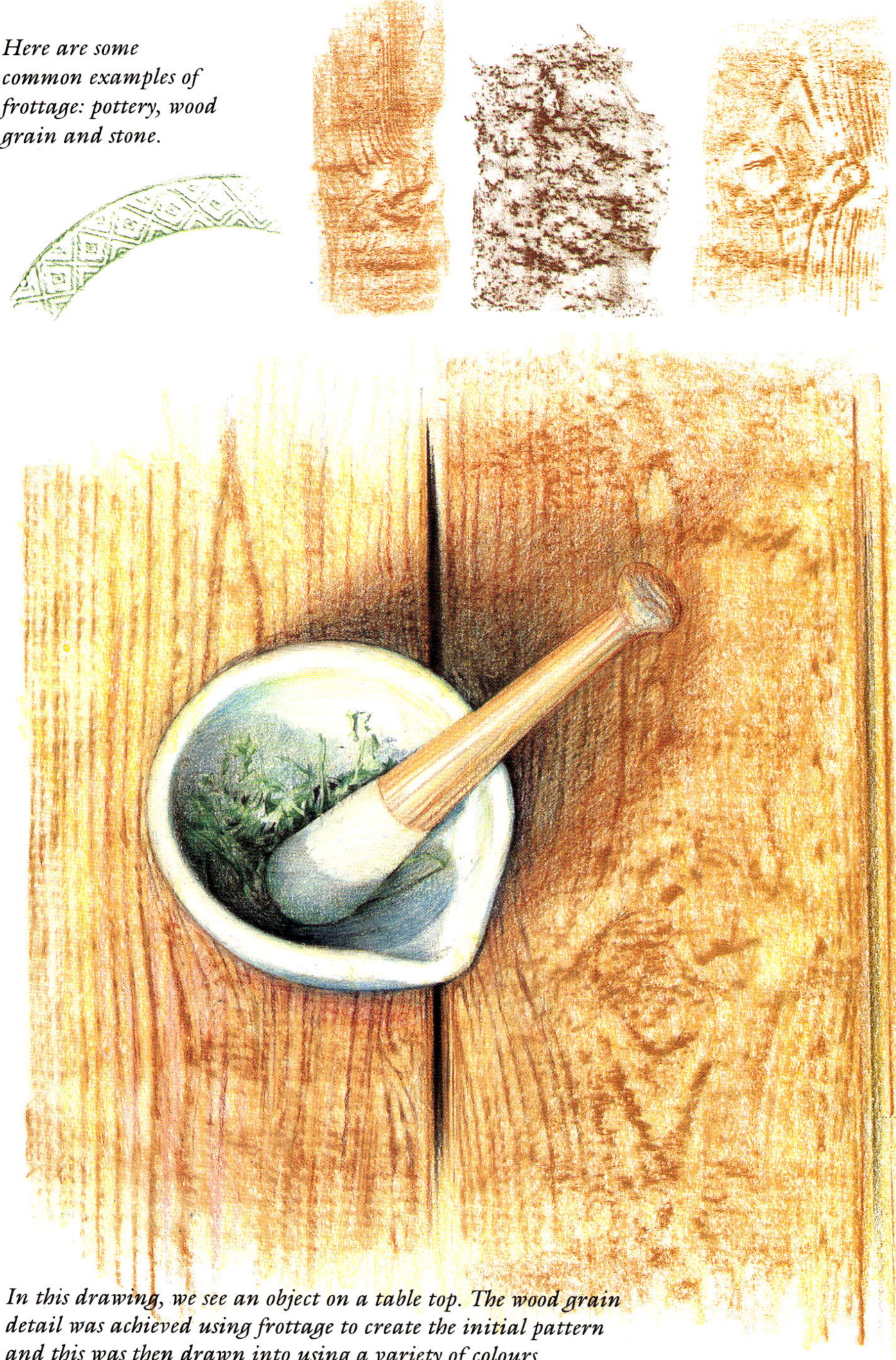

In this drawing, we see an object on a table top. The wood grain detail was achieved using frottage to create the initial pattern and this was then drawn into using a variety of colours.

MASKING

This is a simple but useful method of keeping unwanted colour off areas of your drawing where it is not required. A mask can be anything from a simple piece of cut or torn paper, masking tape or specially manufactured masking film (a thin sheet of clear plastic with a 'low tack' sticky surface on one side), which is laid over the drawing. The areas you wish to draw through are then cut out.

Using paper that has been cut or torn into the shape you want can give a good clean edge if the mask is held steady, but if it is moved slightly from time to time during the shading process, a nicely softened edge will be produced. You will find that using a mask in this way is an invaluable aid, allowing you to create edges and shapes while drawing freely and quickly over them. It avoids working laboriously on those edges, and enables you to achieve that much strived-for free quality.

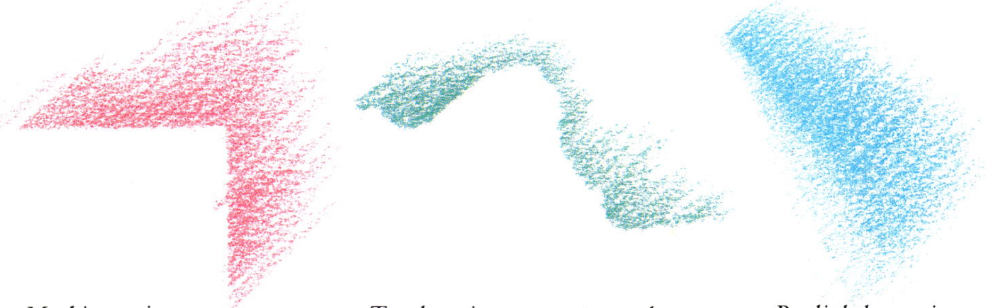

Masking using a cut paper mask giving a precise clean edge.

Try drawing over a torn edge which will produce a softer feel to your work.

By slightly moving a torn mask a feathered edge is created.

Masking tape provides a more rigid effect and is good when a straight edge is required. Care should be taken not to press too hard on the tape as it can sometimes be difficult to remove.

Masking film allows you to mask off quite intricate areas within a picture. It can be used at the beginning of a drawing to assist blocking in various areas of colour or later in the process to protect existing work from being drawn over.

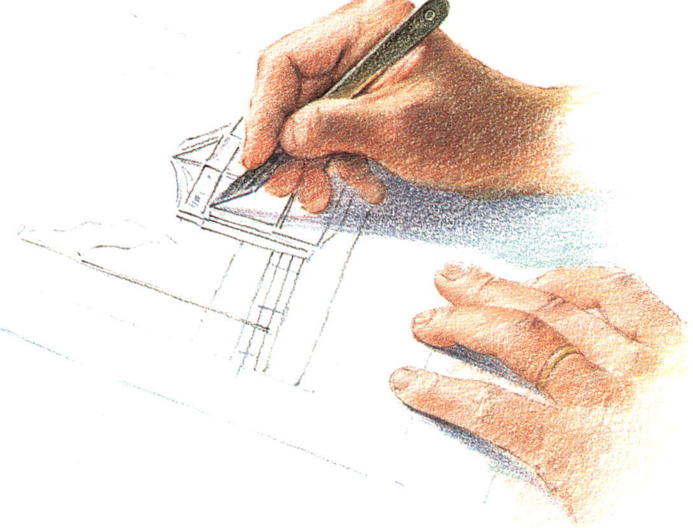

Clear low tack masking film is placed over your initial line drawing, then the areas to be drawn through are very carefully cut out, revealing the paper surface. Very precise effects can be achieved using this technique.

USING AN ERASER

Erasers and knife blades can be useful tools for blending colour and making tonal adjustments, as well as for removing unwanted passages of drawing. Experimenting with various types of eraser will help you discover what each one can do. I find a kneaded eraser the most useful for removing any excess of colour without smudging the surface.

When it comes to removing colour tonally, this requires a combination of first removing the excess with a kneaded eraser, then removing as much as possible with a plastic or rubber eraser, and finally gently scraping off any stains with a scalpel blade.

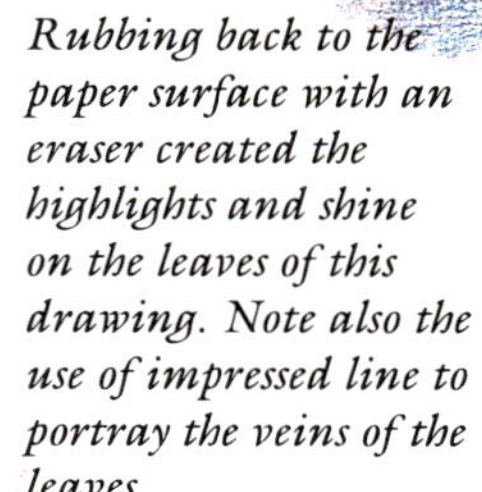

Rubbing back to the paper surface with an eraser created the highlights and shine on the leaves of this drawing. Note also the use of impressed line to portray the veins of the leaves.

PATCH CORRECTIONS

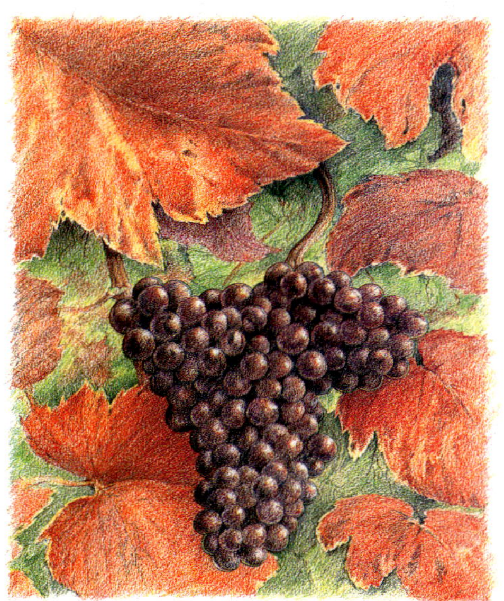

There are times when part of a drawing can become tired and overworked and trying to remove it with an eraser just seems to make it worse. If the rest of the drawing is working, it is often not necessary to completely scrap the whole thing.

A patch correction can be made which, if done with care, should be almost invisible. This is done by placing a clean sheet of paper (of the same grade as the paper your drawing is on) under the area to be corrected, then cutting around the fault – trying as far as possible to follow any hard edges within the picture and so hiding the knife marks.

Great care must be taken when deciding which areas are to be removed when making a patch correction. Always plan out the route your knife will take before you begin cutting. Use a blade with a very thin sharp point, keep it upright and cut through both sheets of paper first time. Gently remove the unwanted section, tape in the clean sheet and you're ready to go!

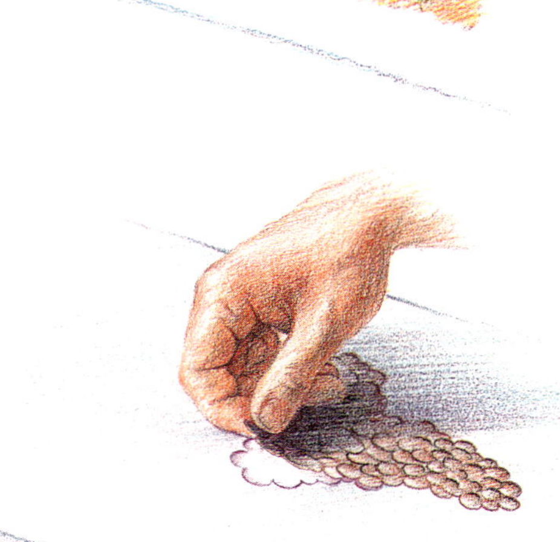

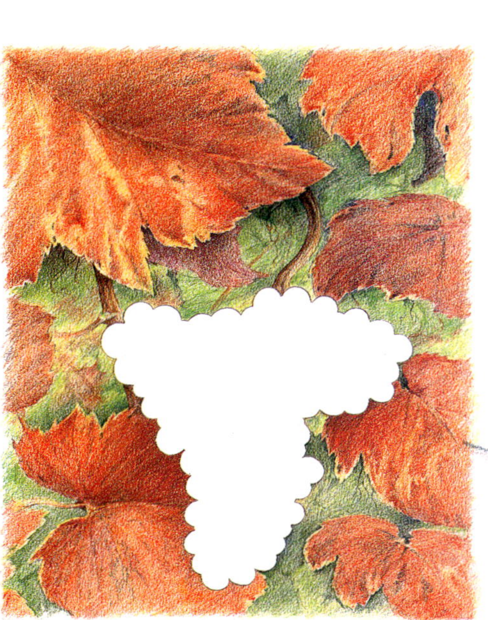

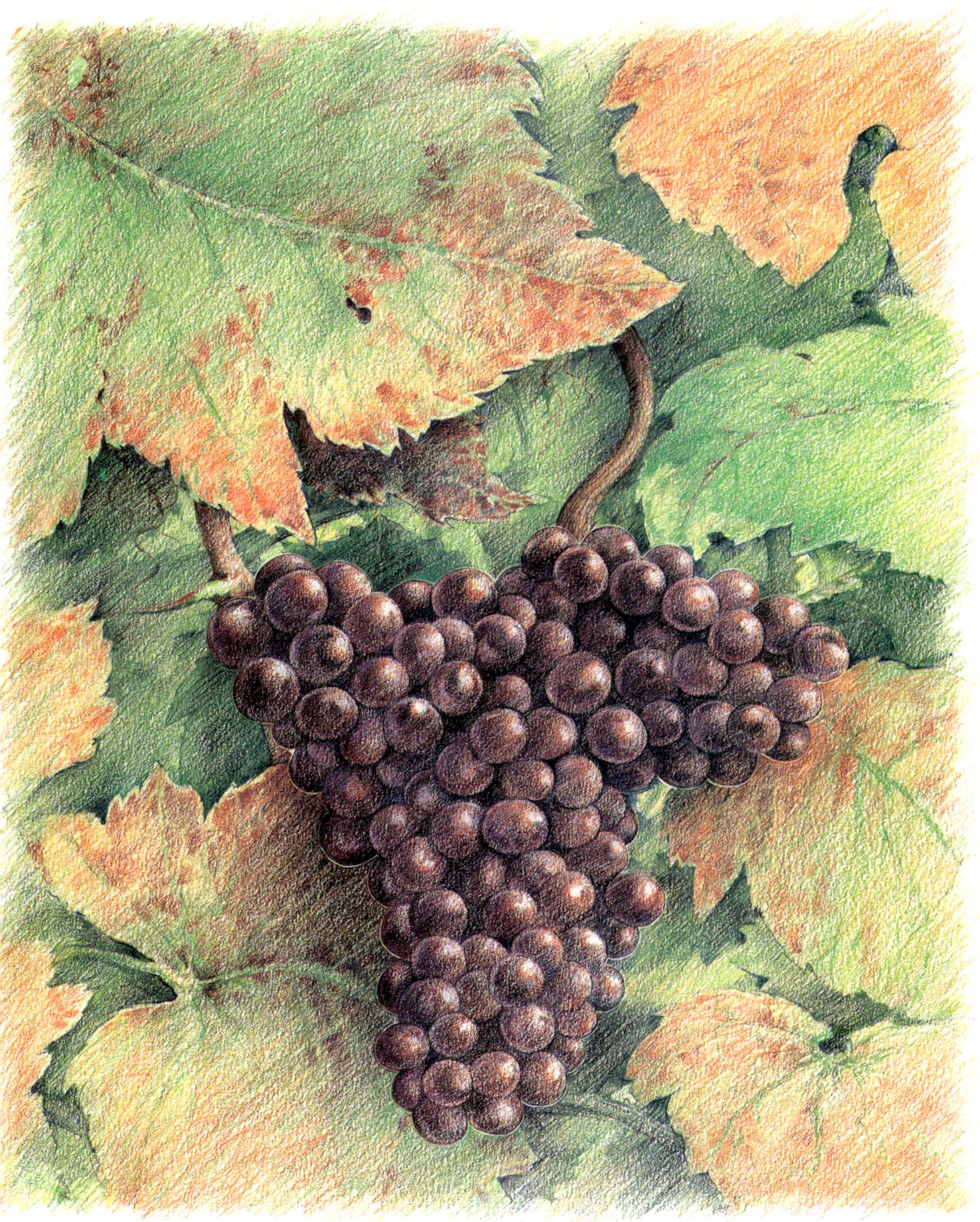

I made a patch correction to this drawing by cutting with a scalpel blade around the edge of the grapes. I then placed them on a fresh sheet of paper, allowing me to redraw the vine leaves in a different colour.

Make sure you cut through both sheets; in this way, a clean patch of exactly the right shape and size is made from the bottom sheet. All that remains to be done is to tape this new patch into place from behind. You can then begin reworking.

TINTED PAPER

Working on tinted paper has a profound influence and, used correctly, can have distinct advantages in bringing unity to an image and acting as a mid tone into which dark tones recede and out of which highlights can be drawn. This is very different from working on white paper, where the white of the surface acts as the highlight, all other tonal values receding from there. The tint of the paper has a marked effect on the appearance of the colour, the exact same colour drawn on to differently tinted paper will appear quite changed.

Bearing this in mind, great care should be taken over choosing colours when working on tinted grounds or you may get something other than what you bargained for. Making colour charts is the only way to discover what these effects will be.

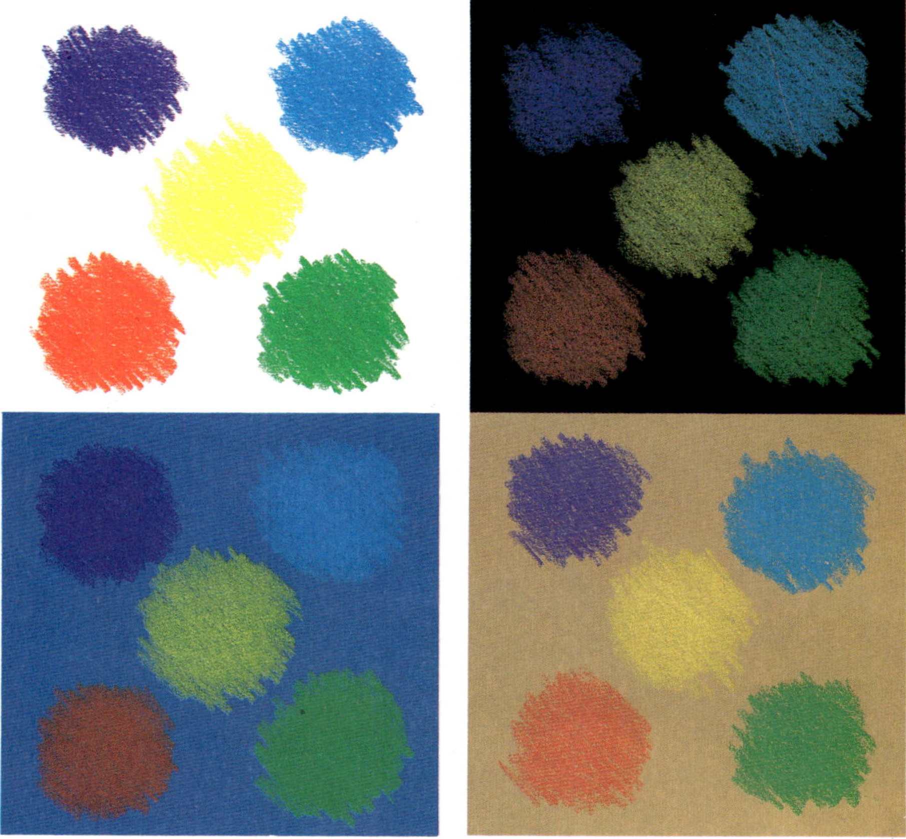

These colour samples on various tinted papers show the influence of the surface colour on a given hue, when applied over it.

MIX AND MATCH

All these techniques can be used with all types of coloured pencil and indeed the various kinds of pencil can all be mixed together to great effect. Using water-soluble pencils as a watercolour wash, drawing into that with a range of chalk, pastel and wax pencil can be great fun and produce spectacular results. So don't be afraid to mix and match your medium and see where it takes you.

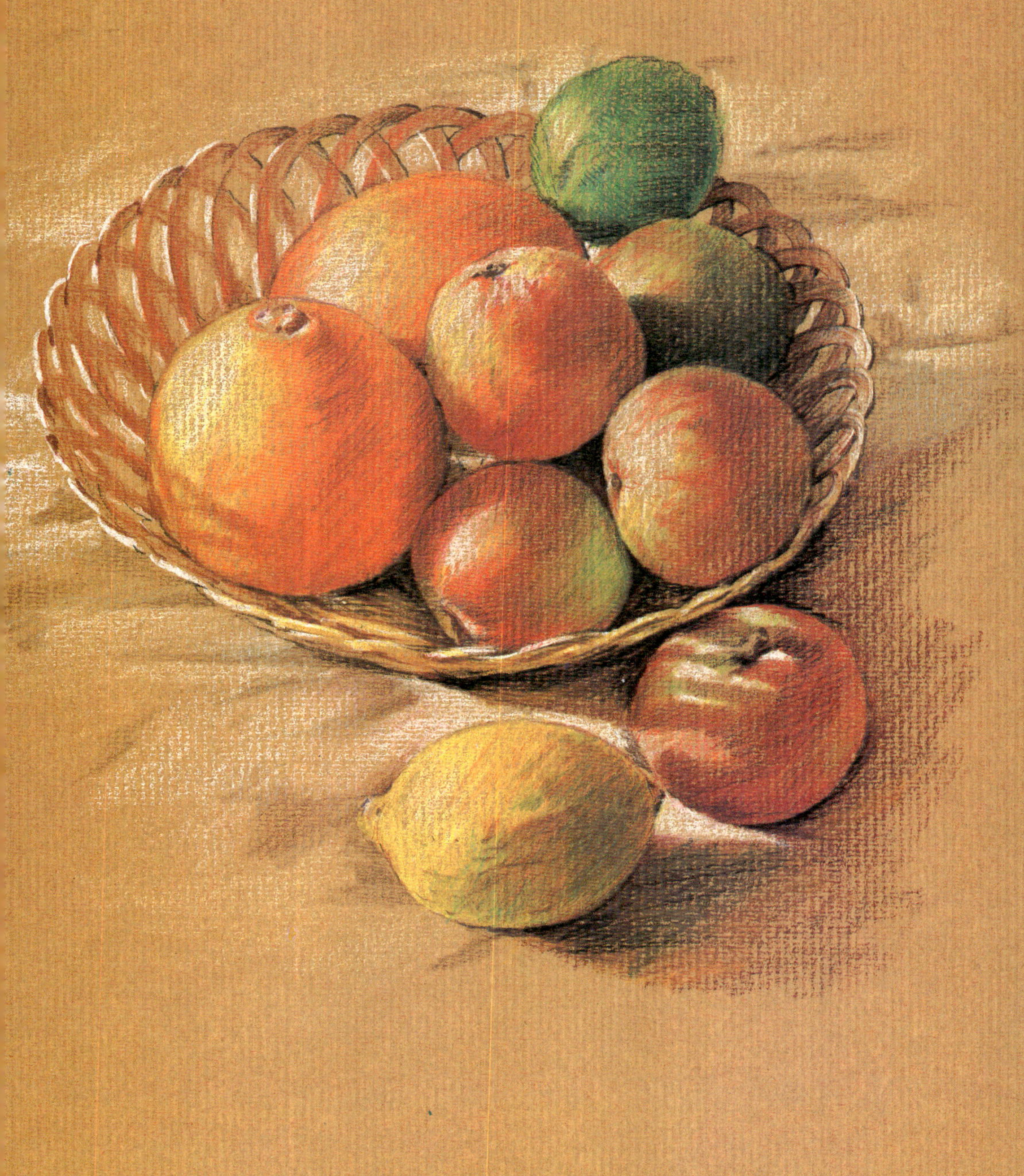

The sienna tint on this paper brings a sunny warmth to this simple still life.

COLOUR

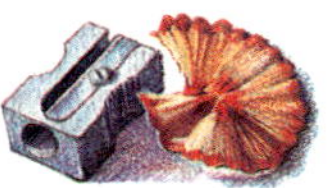

COLOUR IS A FASCINATING AND complicated subject which, in a book of this size, it is simply not possible to cover comprehensively. It is important, however, to cover the basic rules.

For artistic purposes, colour is said to have three characteristics: hue, tonal value and intensity.

The hue of a colour is the word used to describe it – red, blue, green, etc.

The tonal value of a colour is the degree of lightness or darkness measured on a neutral scale from black to white.

The intensity of a colour is said to be its degree of brightness. A colour is usually at its most intense when it is pure, unmixed and saturated on to the surface.

Artists see colour in terms of warm and cold, with varying degrees in between. The hues tending towards the reds and yellows are warm, with those tending towards the blues being cold.

As a rule of thumb, warm colours will come out towards you and cool ones will tend to recede. This aspect of colour is most obviously exploited in landscape pictures to help create the illusion of great space. Cool distant views lost in the ether, with warm more tangible objects closer to the viewer.

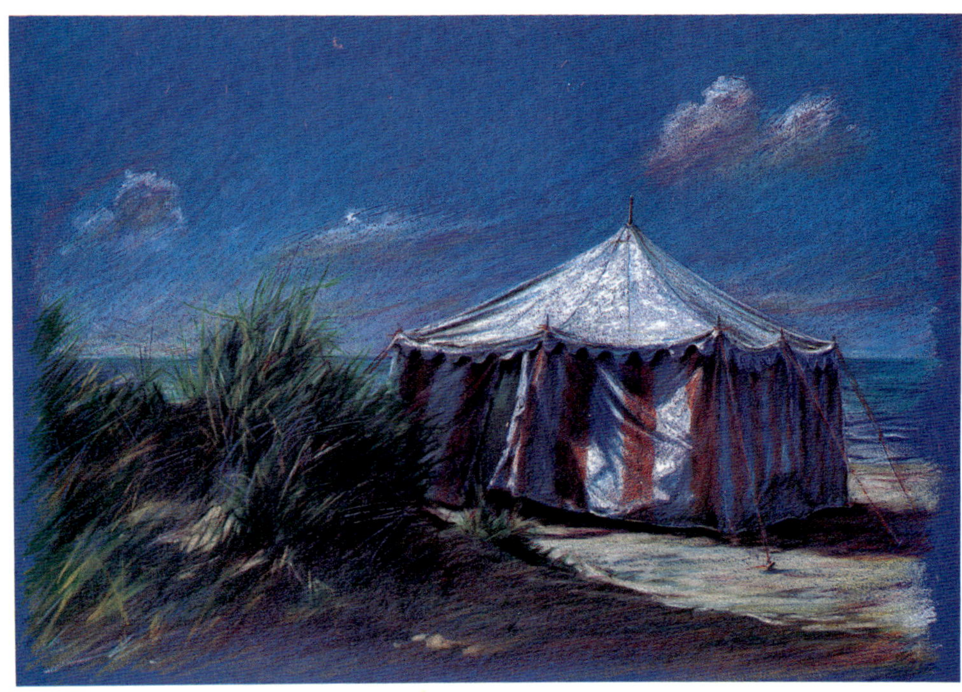

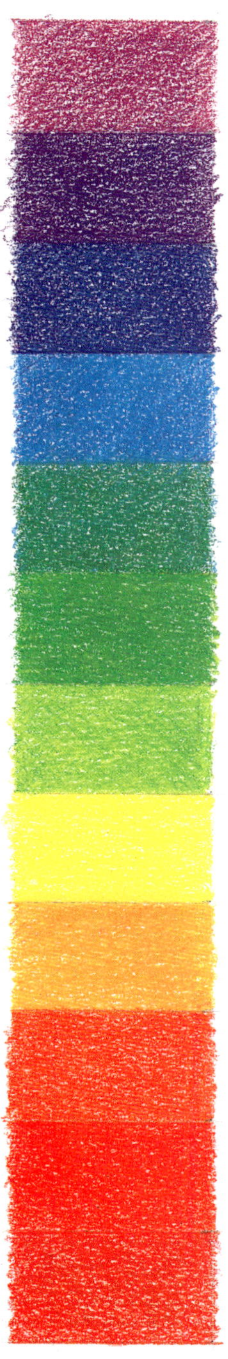

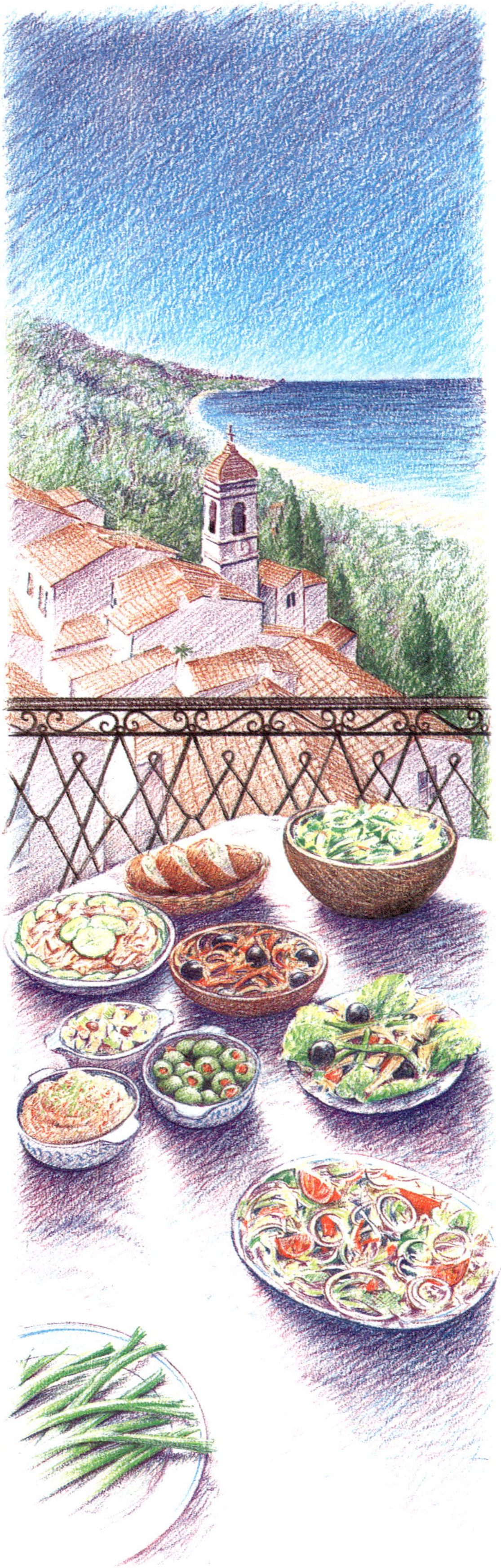

Left *'Marquee on the beach'.
The drawing opposite was
made on blue paper
enhancing the blueness of sky
and ocean, also giving
contrast to the white canvas of
the marquee.*
Right *A sense of space and
scale is created by using cold
hues in the distance and
warm colours in the
foreground.*

COLOUR WHEEL

There are three primary colours: blue, red and yellow. Each of the primary colours is indivisible, which means it is not possible to mix them from other hues. All others are made from these three.

A circular colour chart shows the three primary hues with their accompanying secondary colours (mixtures between two neighbouring primaries). And opposite each primary is its complementary secondary colour. For example, opposite red is green (a mixture of blue and yellow). Opposite blue is orange (a mixture of red and yellow). And opposite yellow is violet (a mixture of blue and red).

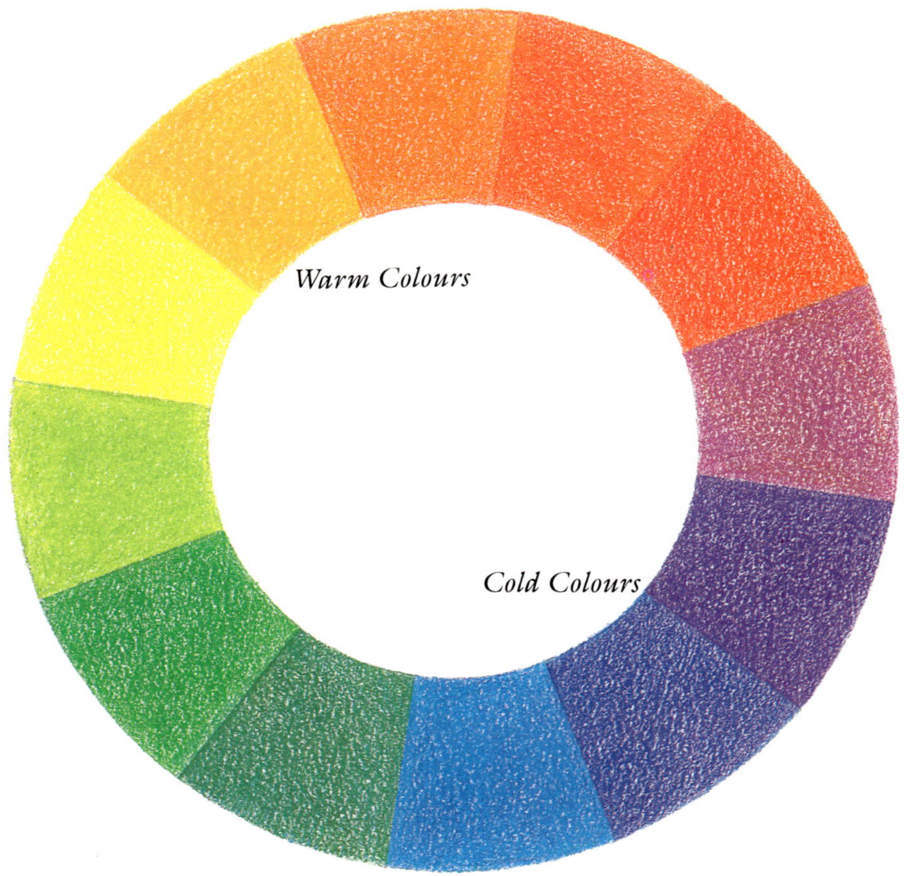

Once again, the way in which the colours are grouped on the chart demonstrates the principle of warm to cold. The hues obtained by mixing elements from all three primaries are collectively known as tertiary colours, of which there is an infinite combination.

With this in mind, you can see that when choosing which colours to use, it is important to achieve a balance of warm and cold. There is a vast array of hues available to artists using coloured pencils. My advice, however, is to resist the temptation to have the complete range from the outset. It can be quite bewildering to have too great a choice.

Limit your palette to begin with, only adding new colours as and when you require them for a specific purpose. In this way, you will acquire the most useful colours, as well as an intimate understanding of what each one is capable of.

Drawings made using only one colour (monochrome), with neutral white and black to provide tonal contrast can be very effective, creating a very particular mood and atmosphere. Too much colour, on the other hand, can sometimes detract from the overall composition and content of a drawing.

As a rule of thumb, if you don't know why you are using a colour then don't use it. If in doubt, leave it out is a wise maxim. Experiment with combinations of colour on rough sheets to discover the effect they have on one another.

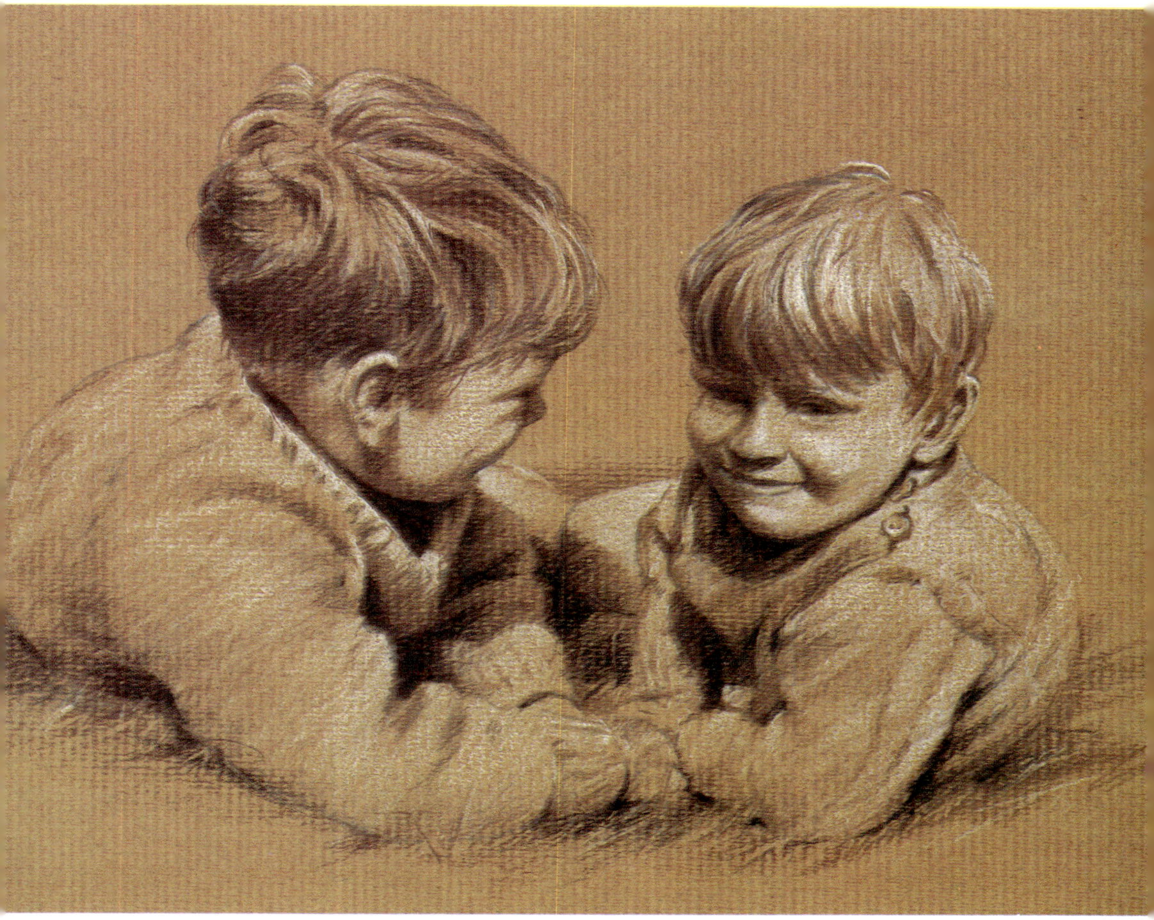

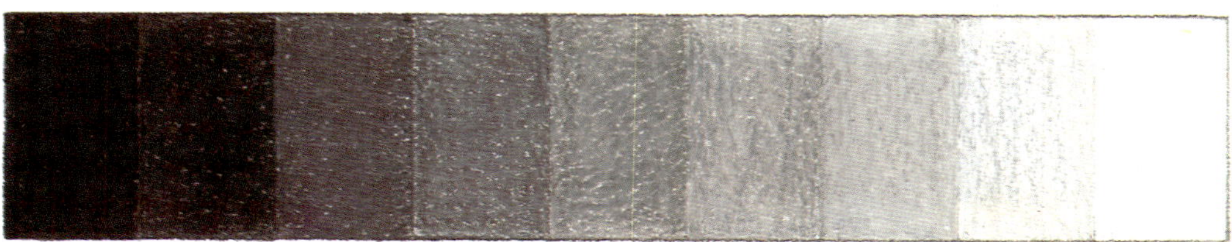

By limiting the palette to monochrome and working on a tinted surface an atmosphere of nostalgia was brought to this drawing, reminiscent of an old photograph.

THEME &
COMPOSITION

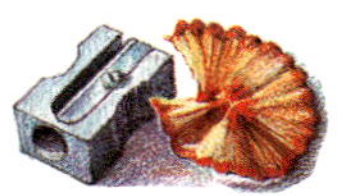

COLOURED PENCILS CAN BE EFFECTIVELY applied to a remarkable range of subjects. Obviously, as with other media, they tend to lend themselves better to certain subjects, but with imagination and some ingenuity it is possible to draw just about anything.

Having chosen your subject, there are several important things to establish before making a start. Preliminary sketches will help you decide on the best approach to the final drawing. They will also improve your drawing skills.

Whatever your subject, certain basic rules always apply. The effect of light is a crucial element in picture making. Strong dynamic light brings drama and intensity to an image; soft diffuse light gives an ethereal, atmospheric feel; unusual sources of light can create sinister undertones; and so on. Where you are in control of these influences, it pays to experiment with the various effects.

Aesthetically pleasing compositions are, to some extent, a matter of individual taste. Generally speaking, however, when composing an image one looks for a 'focal point' to draw the eye into the picture, around which are a number of complementary forces.

As with lighting, the effect of how one crops an image is of paramount importance. A subject viewed from a distance, for example, with lots of space around it will appear remote and isolated. Cropping in hard on the same subject has the opposite effect and will produce a feeling of claustrophobia and intimacy.

By raising or lowering your viewpoint from the conventional straight-on eye level, the drama of a subject can be increased.

Having established all this with your preliminary sketches, you are now ready to make a more refined drawing. With certain subjects, it may not be possible to have them in front of you during the whole period it takes to make a drawing. If your preliminary sketches are good, they should provide you with most of the reference you are going to need, but probably not all.

These strings of onions and garlic hanging on an old barn door, with its rusted hinges and weather beaten surface, made an interesting study of light and texture.

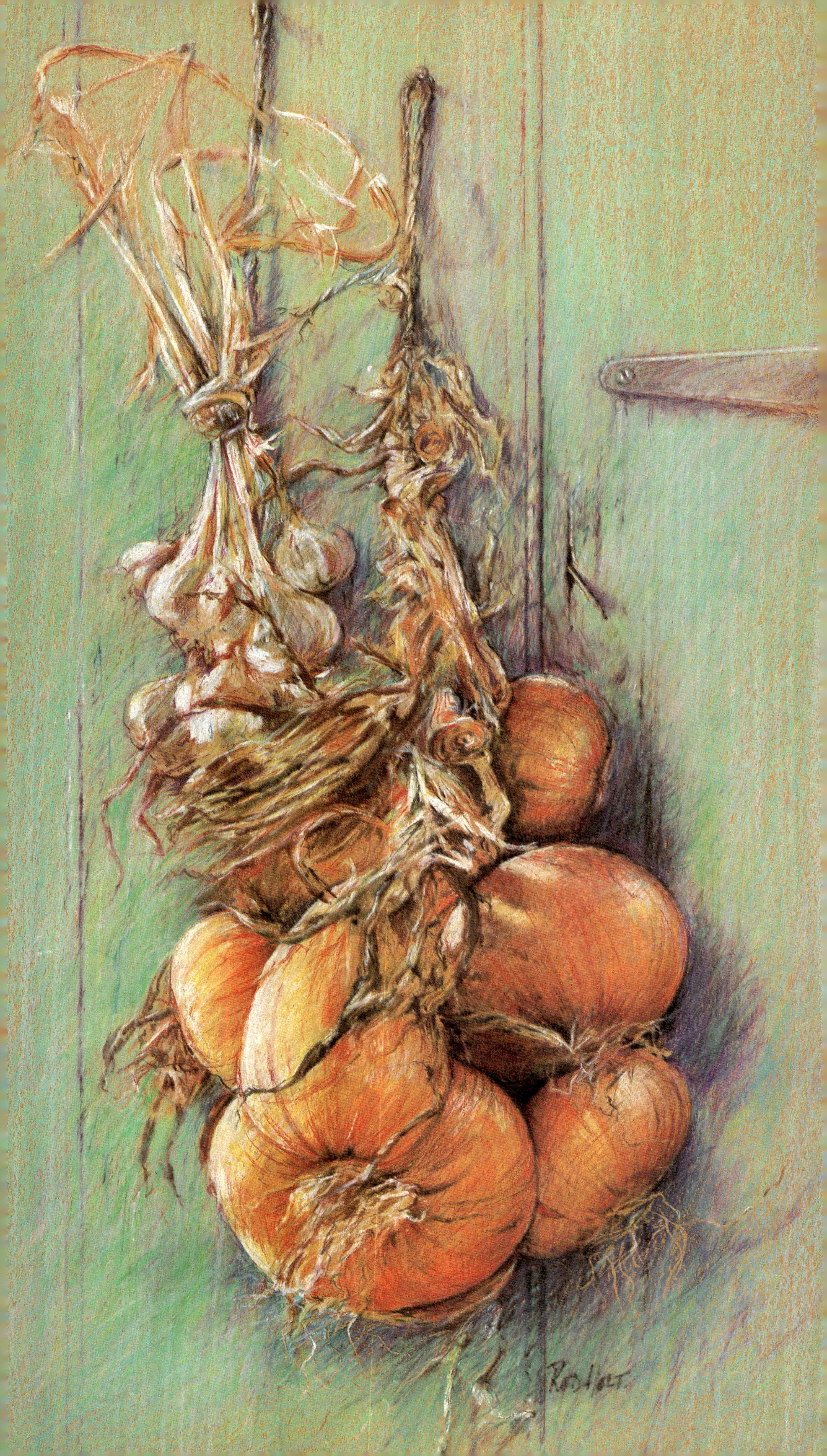

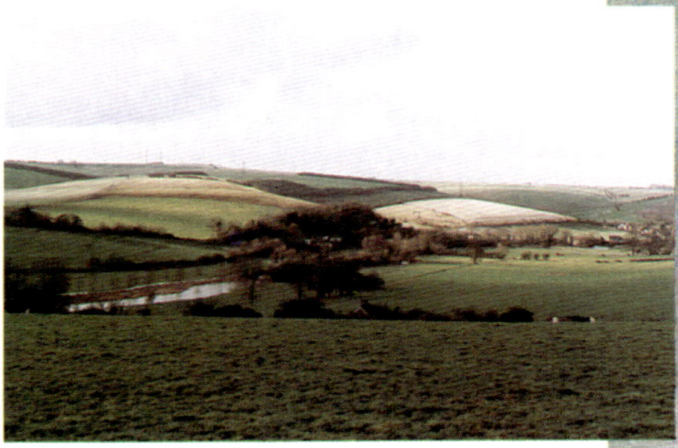

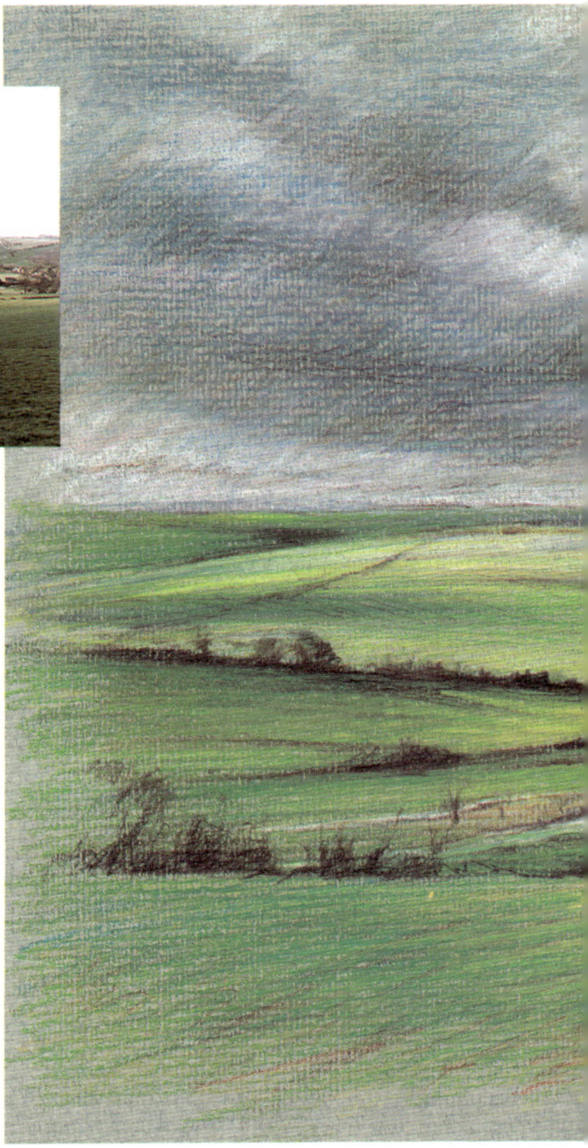

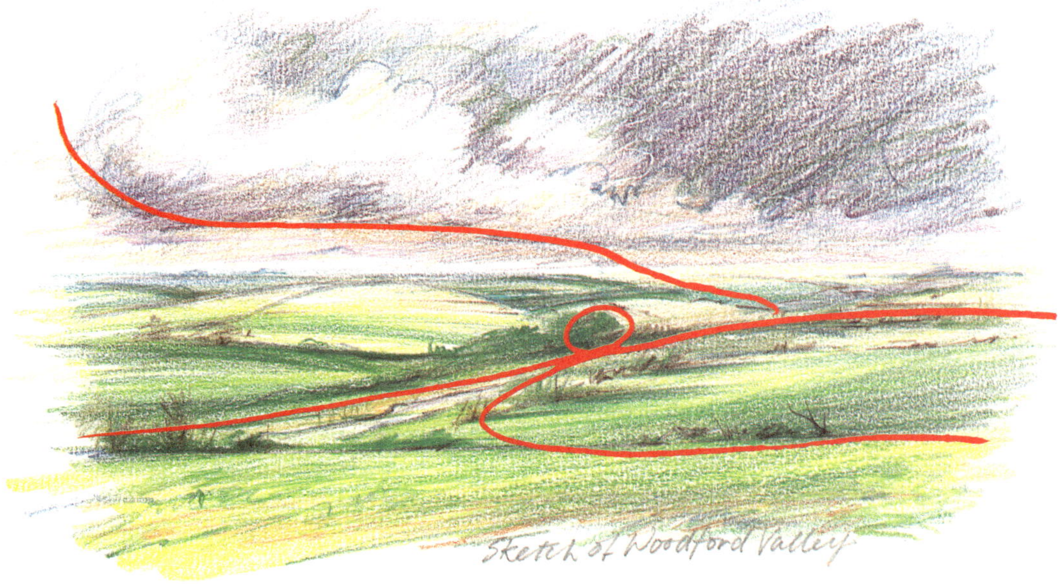

'Sun and clouds over Woodford'.
The knot of trees cradled between
the two sunlit hills form the focal
point of this composition. The
patches of light and shadow add to
the sensation of the clouds
scudding through the sky. Below
we see the preliminary sketch and
above the photograph used as
reference to make the final more
refined image.

Sketch of Woodford Valley

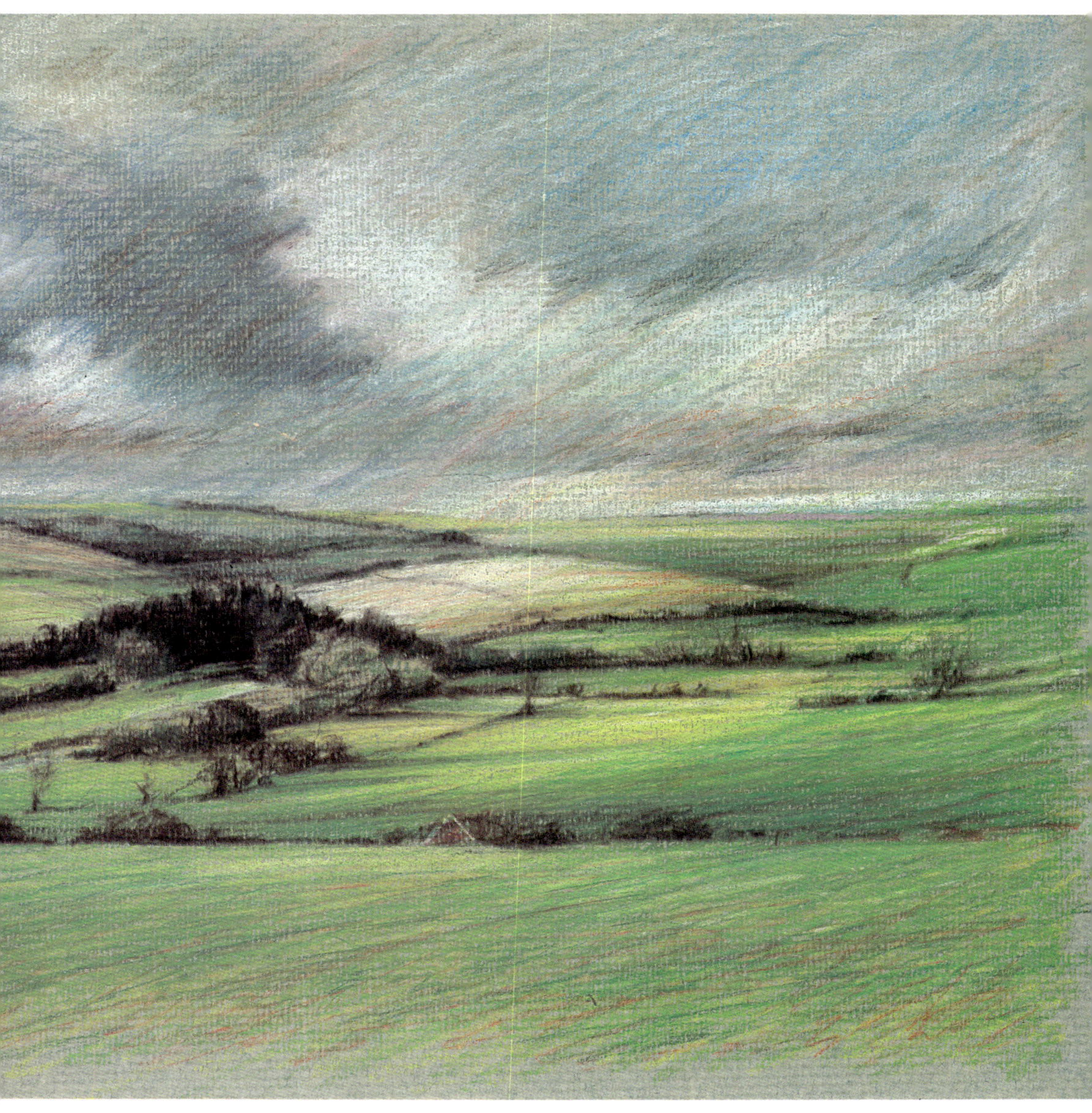

This is where the contentious subject of 'photography' as an artist's aid rears its ugly head. I believe that the camera is an invaluable tool, providing visual references of form, colour and the nature of light in a unique way. Provided one doesn't become a slave to the photograph or try to copy its effects (a worthless pursuit to my mind), it is an undoubted asset. To photograph the head of a child before it moves, for example, or the fugitive nature of light over a landscape before it is lost forever, is tremendously helpful to the artist in need of reference.

STILL LIFE

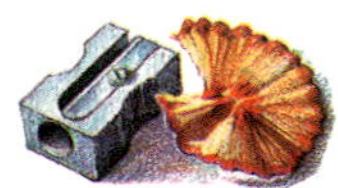

Still life is perhaps the most controllable subject of all, allowing itself to be arranged, rearranged and lit just as the artist wishes. As such, it is very useful for encouraging skills of observation and composition in the beginner. In a practical sense, a group can be set up in an out of the way place and left for as long as is required.

This is not to suggest, though, that still life is only for beginners. Nothing could be further from the truth. Many professional artists who specialise in still life produce some marvellous complete images. There is no need to feel you must graduate on to more difficult areas. Still life drawing can be very rewarding and the choice of subject matter within this all-embracing title is vast.

Simple still lives of everyday objects,
when well lit and carefully composed,
can make very effective pictures.

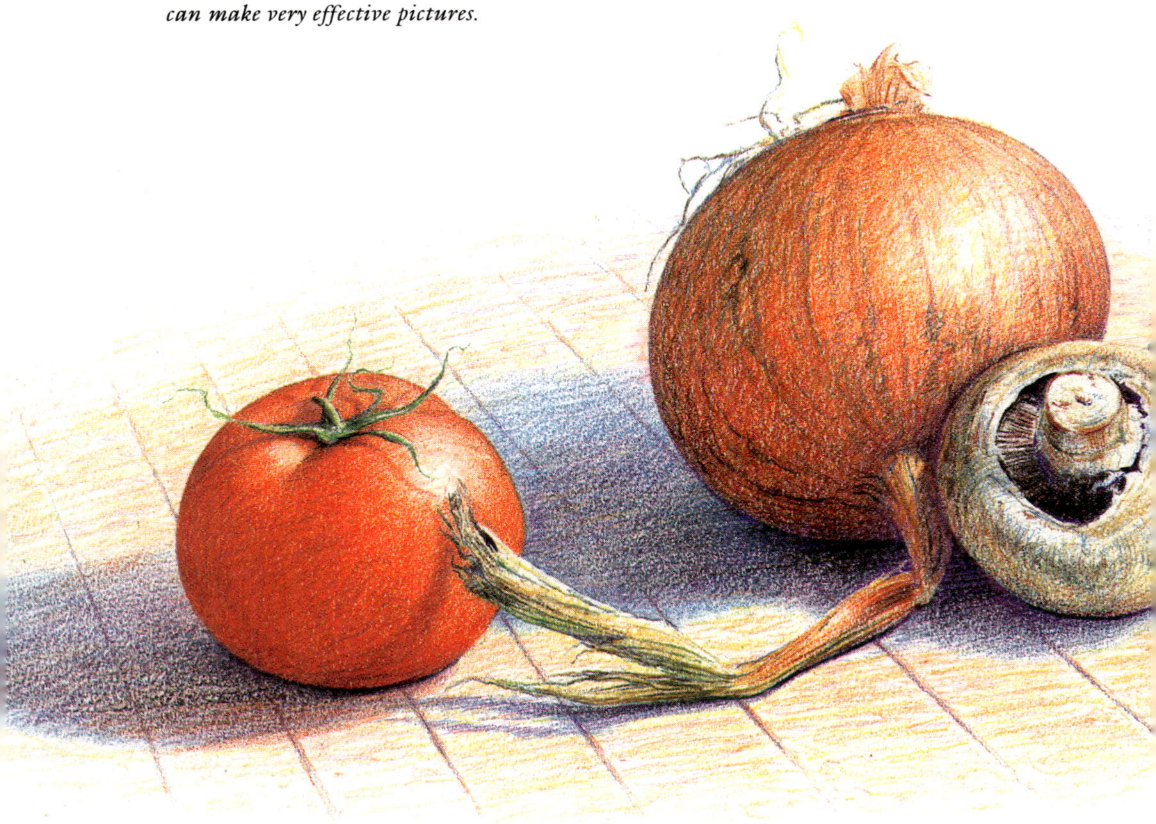

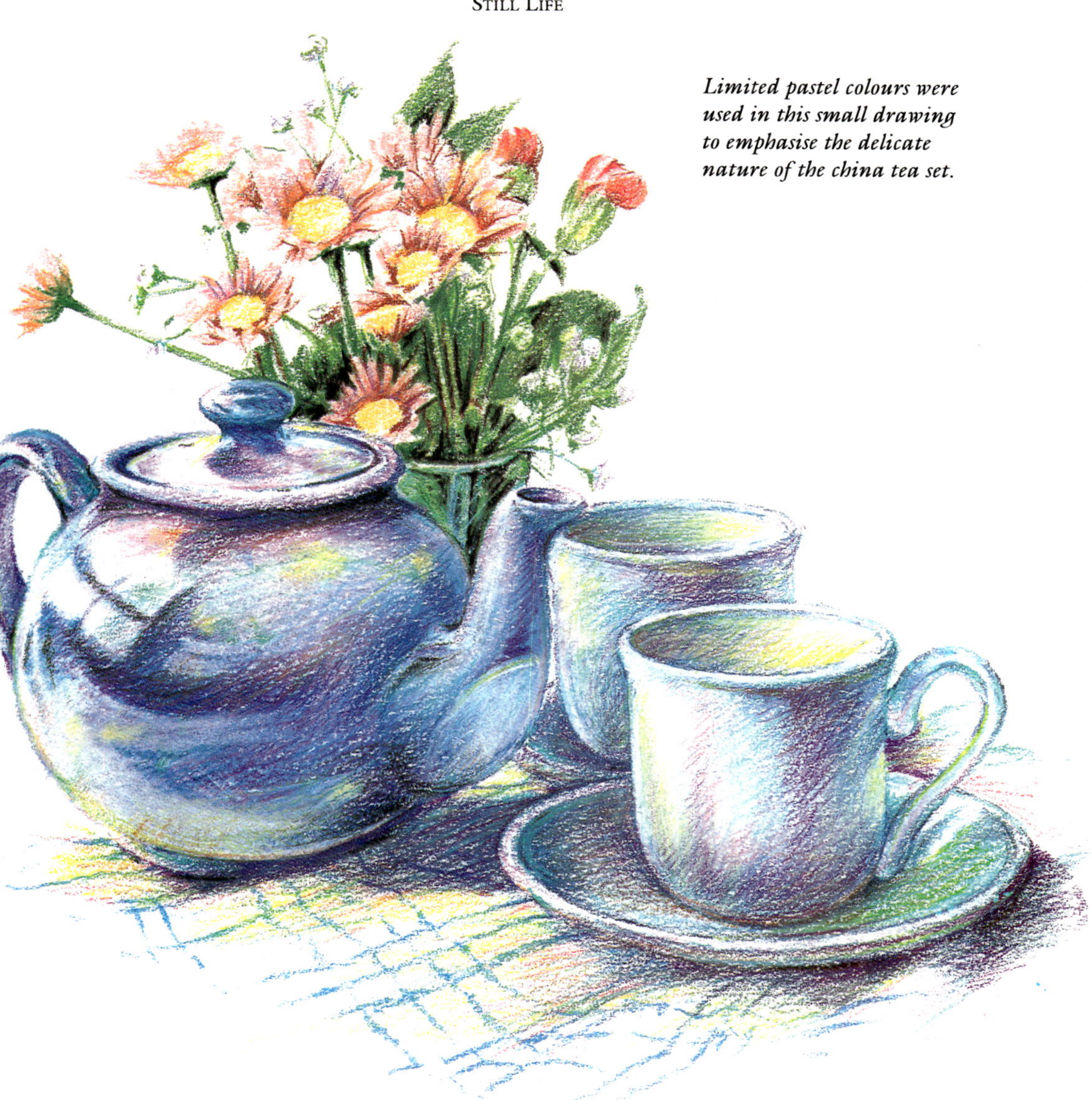

Flowers and fruit are the most obvious and traditional subjects, but
any motionless object you find eye-catching or deem interesting for
some other reason should be considered as the possible subject for a
drawing. It could be the way the light falls over an object or group of
objects on a windowsill, the contents of a jewellery box, lichen
growing on a headstone in a churchyard, or fruit buns on a plate!
Almost anything can be arranged and lit in such a way that will
make it appear pleasing and visually interesting.

During the previous chapter on composition, we explored
the idea of unusual viewpoints and the effects of various
light sources. Here is the opportunity to put theory into
practice. Remember that a still life does not have to be set
on a table and viewed at eye level by the artist sitting in a
chair. Try arranging it on the floor and looking down on it.
Simple, sparse, well-balanced compositions can often be more
striking than cluttered, complicated groups, allowing the subject to have
greater impact.

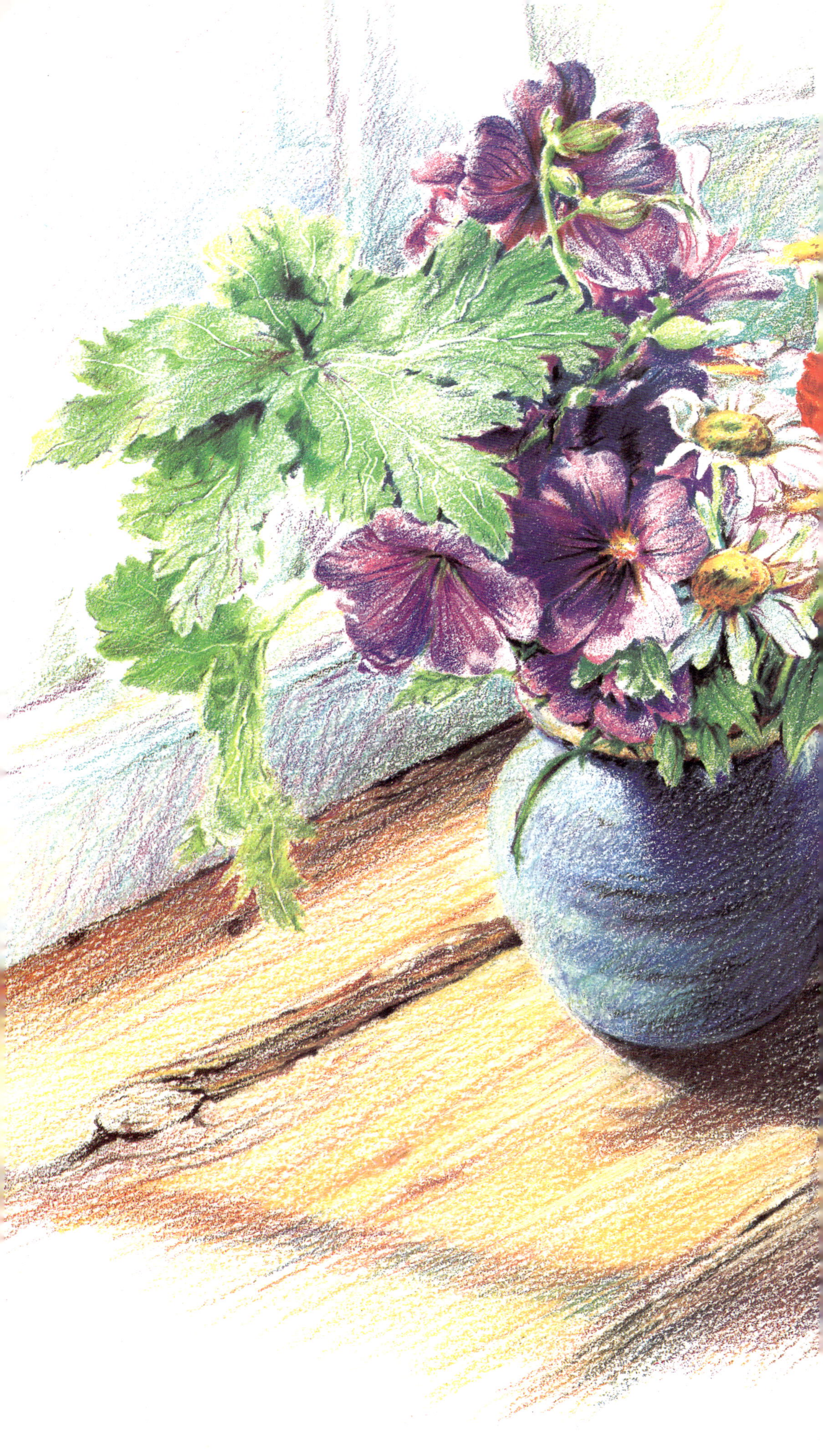

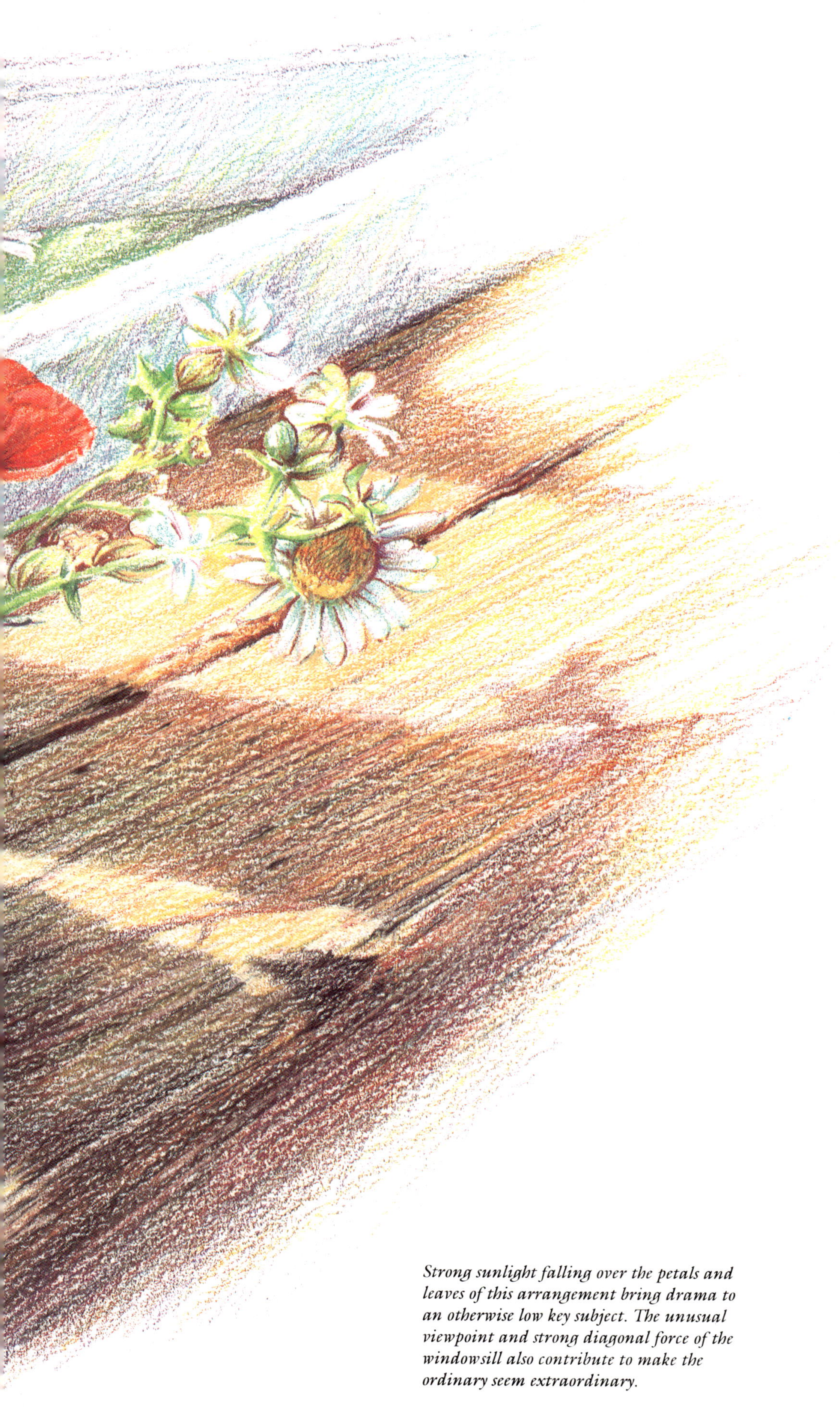

Strong sunlight falling over the petals and leaves of this arrangement bring drama to an otherwise low key subject. The unusual viewpoint and strong diagonal force of the windowsill also contribute to make the ordinary seem extraordinary.

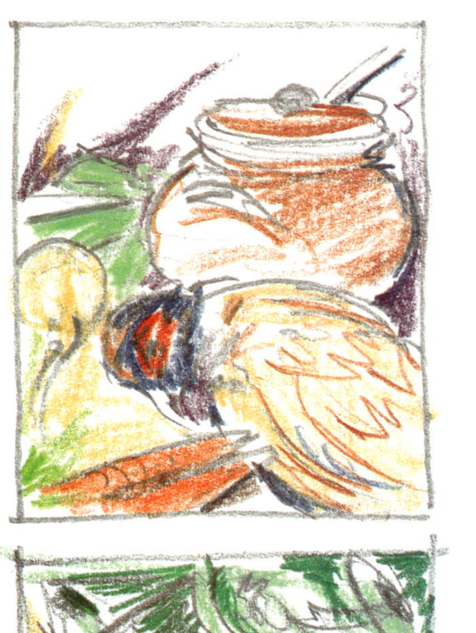
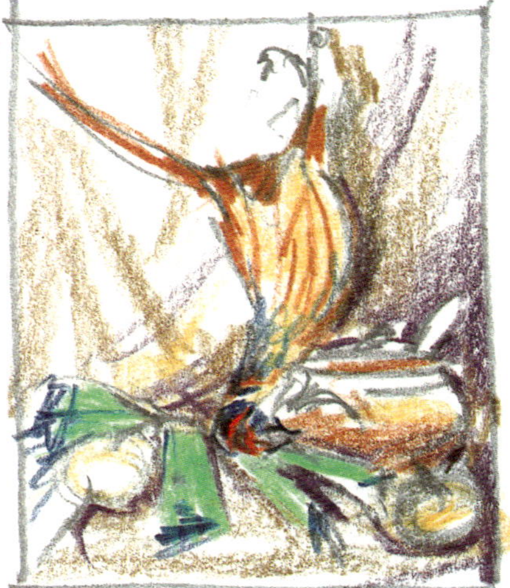
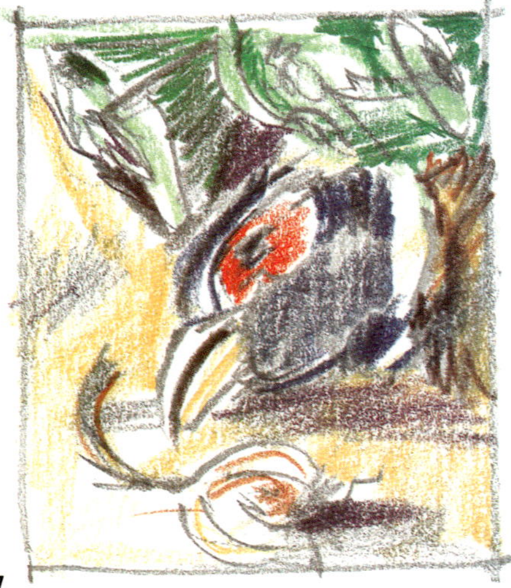
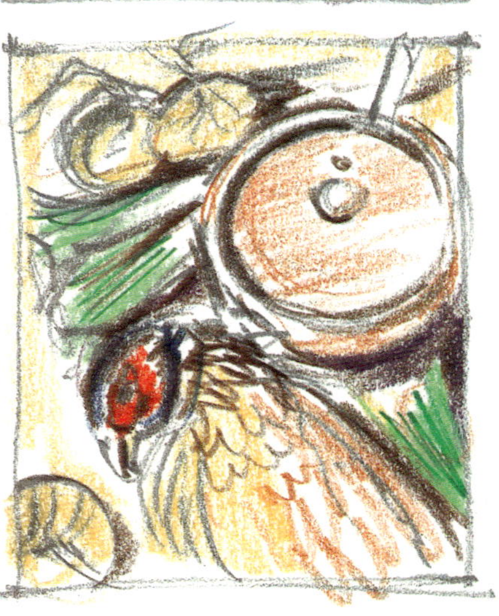

1

1. Setting up: thumbnail sketches establish the viewpoint, the need for close or distant cropping, and the details of the light source.

2. Lay out the whole drawing using light contour lines.
3. Work up the most contrasting tonal areas, giving form to the linear structure and using loose expressive marks at this stage.
Consolidate the tonal areas and colours, refining the marks and defining the shadows.
4. Finally, put in highlights and sharpen up all the little details.

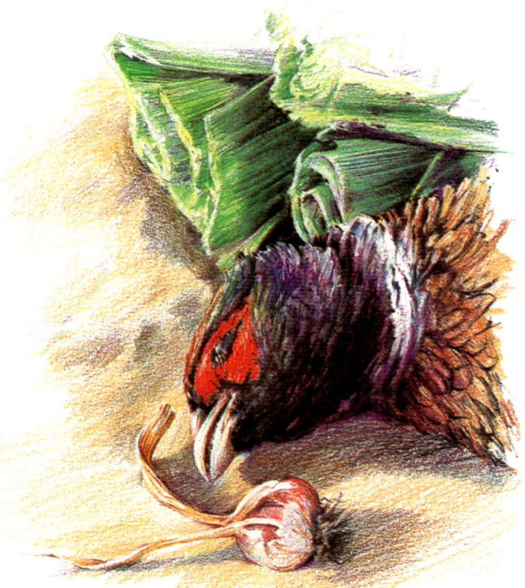

Left. *In this little colour study we can see how sgraffito can be successfully used to portray something such as the feathers of the pheasant's head and the veins on the leeks.*

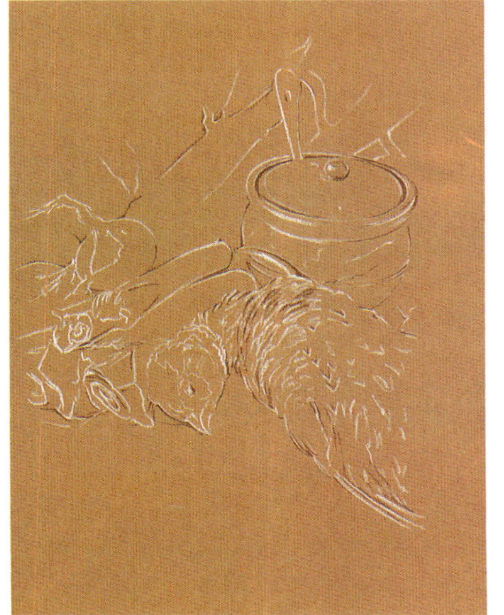

2

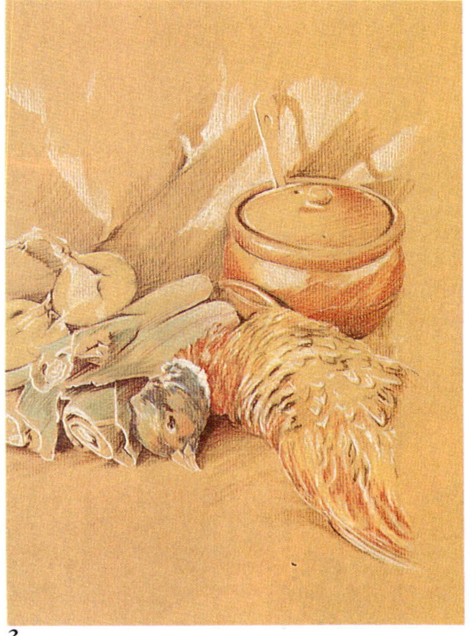

3

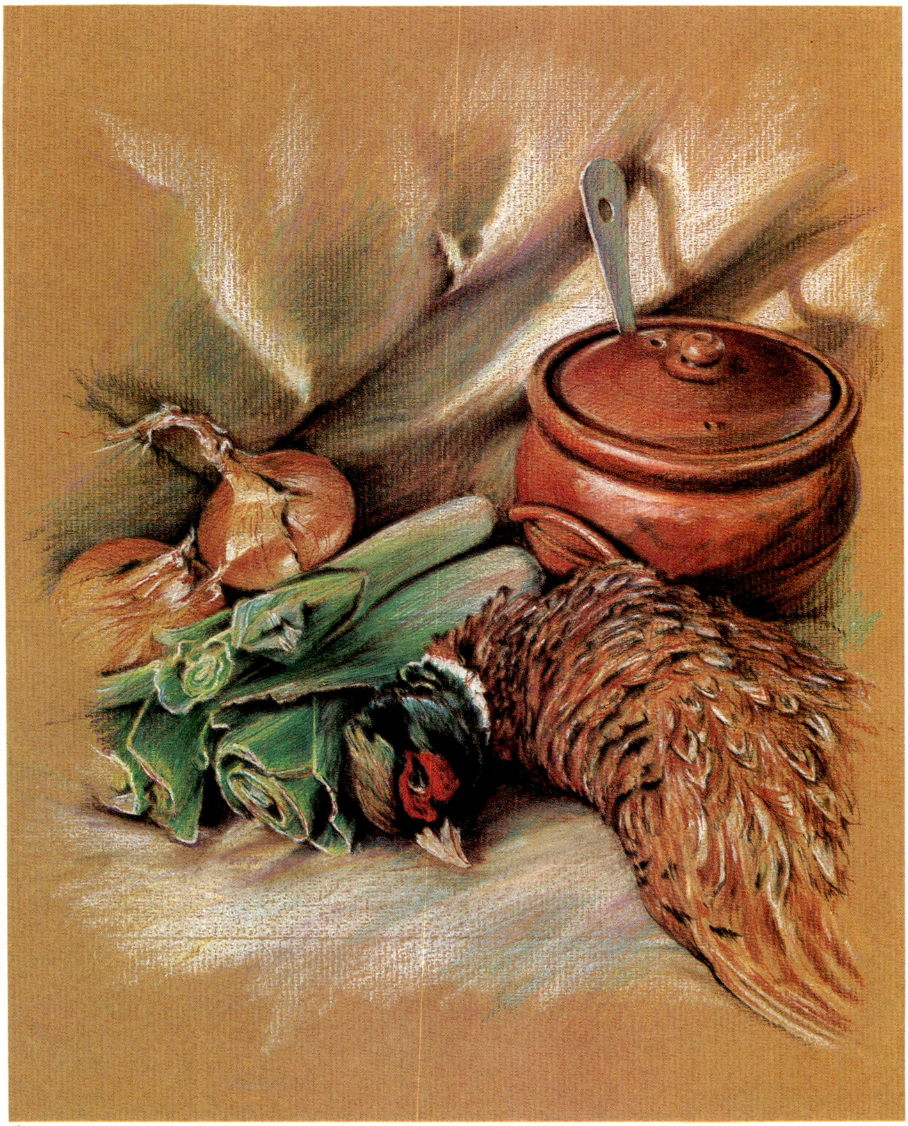

4

LANDSCAPE

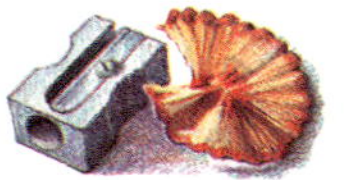

Title ABSOLUTELY VAST SUBJECT OF landscape and your interpretation
of it is a highly personal matter – perhaps more so than any other
area of picture making. One person may look at a scene with the eye of
the impressionist and see a mass of light and colour. Another person,
looking at exactly the same scene, may be drawn into the myriad details
of nature. Whatever your perception of the landscape, to portray it
successfully it is essential to spend time in it, observing the effects of
light and weather.

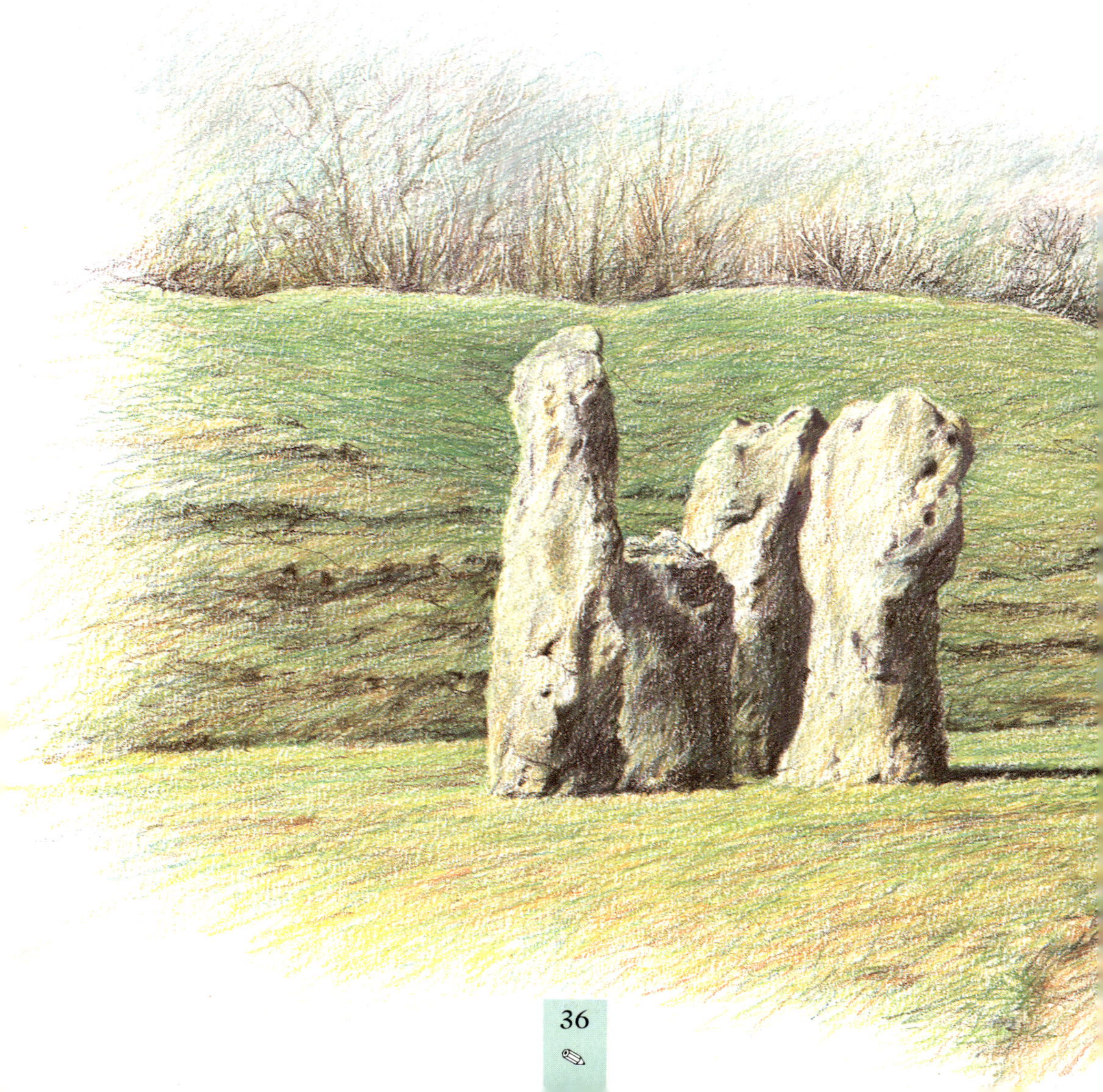

It is not always necessary – or, indeed, possible – to make finished drawings on site. But there is no substitute for getting out and gathering as much information as possible. Use colour sketches and perhaps your own photographs, if you wish.

Plenty of good reference is the name of the game. When drawing out of doors, I use a portable folding seat easel, sheets of cartridge pinned to a light rigid board. A small pocket-sized sketch pad is also useful.

Large-scale landscapes rendered in coloured pencils are very challenging and can be extremely labour intensive. Covering large open areas of sky or land with the point of a pencil can be a laborious matter. Using softer pencils, chalks and pastels helps avoid this. Tinted papers are also very useful for establishing broad areas of colour, and so help to speed up the process. When making studies of the transient nature of light, you need to work fast, using broad gestural marks that capture the essence of a scene. Back in the studio, these can then be refined or used as reference for more complete drawings.

When considering a landscape, it is interesting to note the effect that placing an object, building or figure in it can have. A scene containing a single distant figure often appears more desolate and isolated than a completely empty landscape.

*'Standing stones'. Once again strong
sunlight has enhanced the dramatic effect of
this subject. We see a group of prehistoric
standing stones posed like actors on a stage,
picked out by the strong light against a dark
brooding backdrop.*

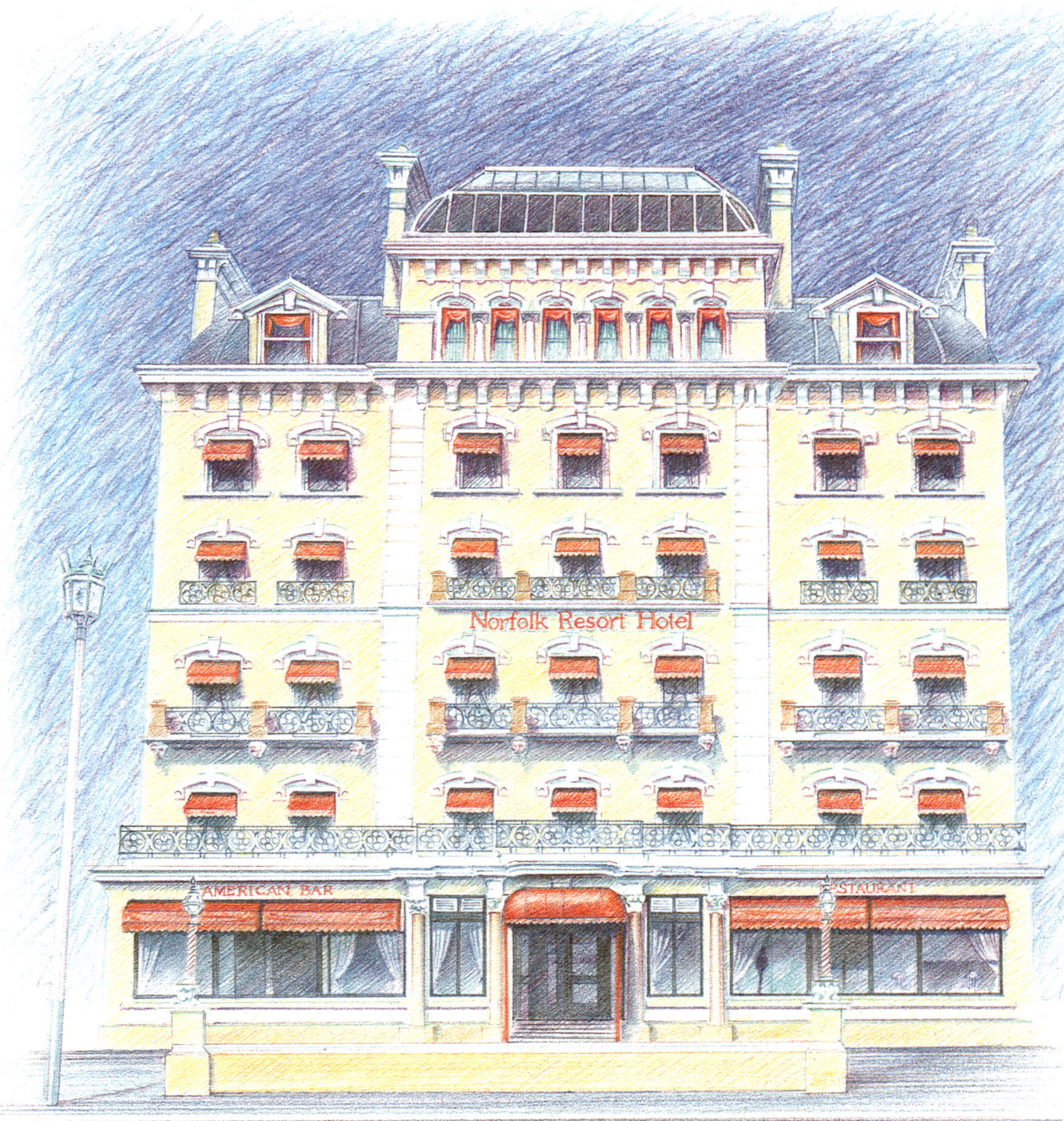

'Norfolk Resort Hotel'. This imposing hotel front totally dominates this composition, viewed face on, towering up white against the strong blue sky. Notice how the sky has been rendered using a myriad of loose scribbled marks, adding vibrancy to the drawing surface.

A building or object of some kind in the composition – whether close or far away – will provide a focal point for the eye to fix on. Such elements help establish a sense of scale and distance, combined with the use of warm and cold colours as described in the chapter on colour.

When you observe a landscape, you are confronted with an enormous quantity of information, which you must quickly break down and simplify. Looking through half-closed eyes helps to assess the most important elements, doing away with all the unwanted details to begin with. In the following step-by-step, you will see how to start by blocking in these elements and only adding selected details later.

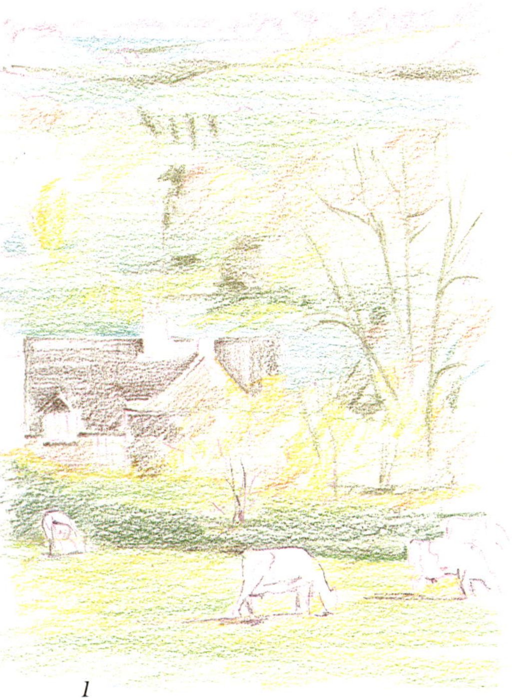

1

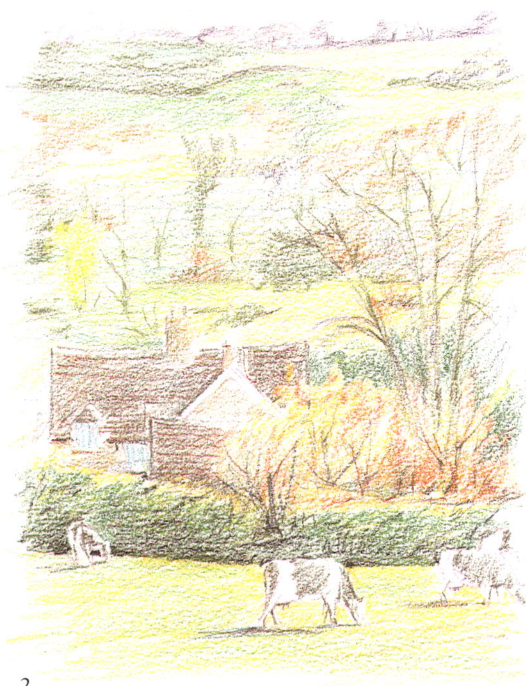

2

1. *Use half-closed eyes to assess the essentials; block in the most important aspects.*
2. *Refine colours, tones and shadows.*
3. *Add final details to bring the whole picture to life.*

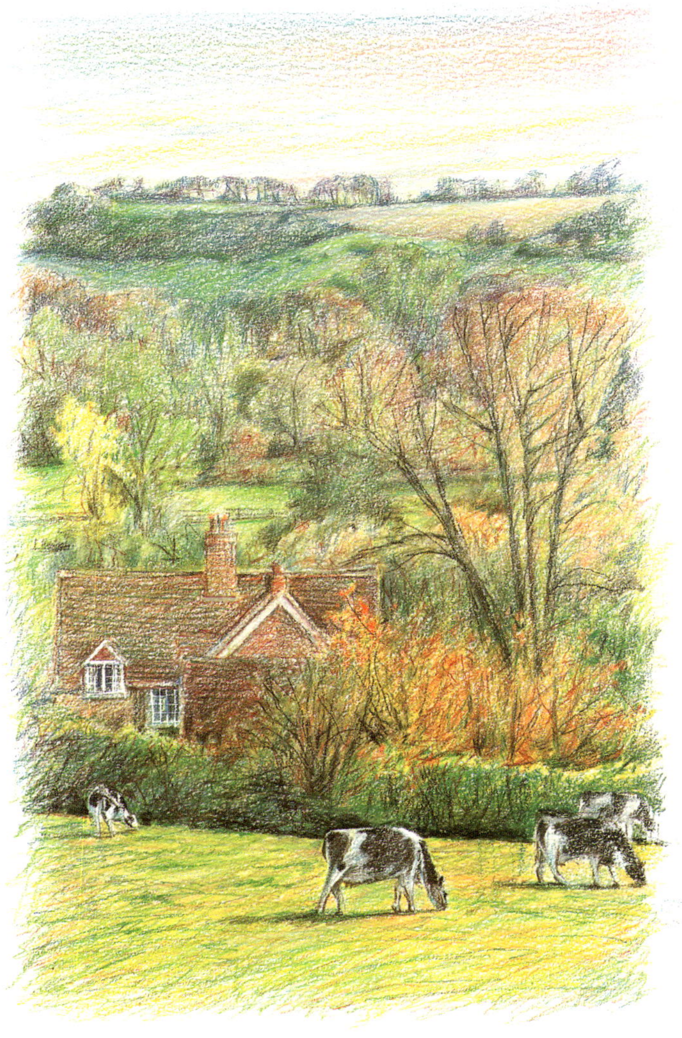

3

PERSPECTIVE

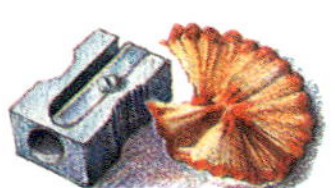

MANY BEGINNERS ARE DAUNTED BY the prospect of making drawings with complicated perspective in them, consequently limiting their choice of subject tremendously. These fears can soon be overcome with the knowledge of a few basic principles, all compositions fitting into a handful of simple constant rules.

Perspective is the method artists use to suggest three dimensions on a two dimensional surface, evoking the sensation of space and distance in a picture. The horizon is at your eye level and any object within view on a flat receding plane, depending on its distance from the viewer, will appear to reduce in size, eventually disappearing at the vanishing point on the horizon (**fig.1**).

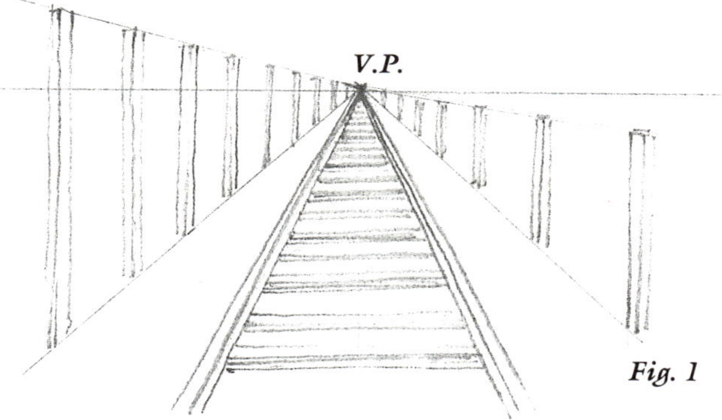

A pair of parallel lines like a train track will appear to converge as they recede into the distance, meeting on the horizon at the vanishing point.

Fig. 1

When drawing buildings, it is necessary to establish the underlying structure of the architecture, seeing them as a block or series of blocks, ignoring any peripheral elements to begin with. In most cases, a second vanishing point will be required on the same horizon, the position determined by your relationship to the subject (**figs. 2 & 3**).

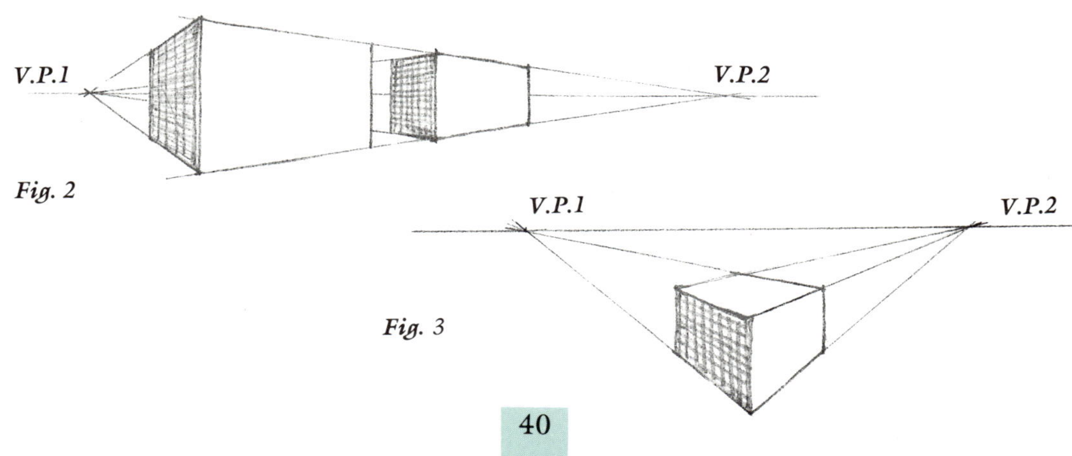

Fig. 2

Fig. 3

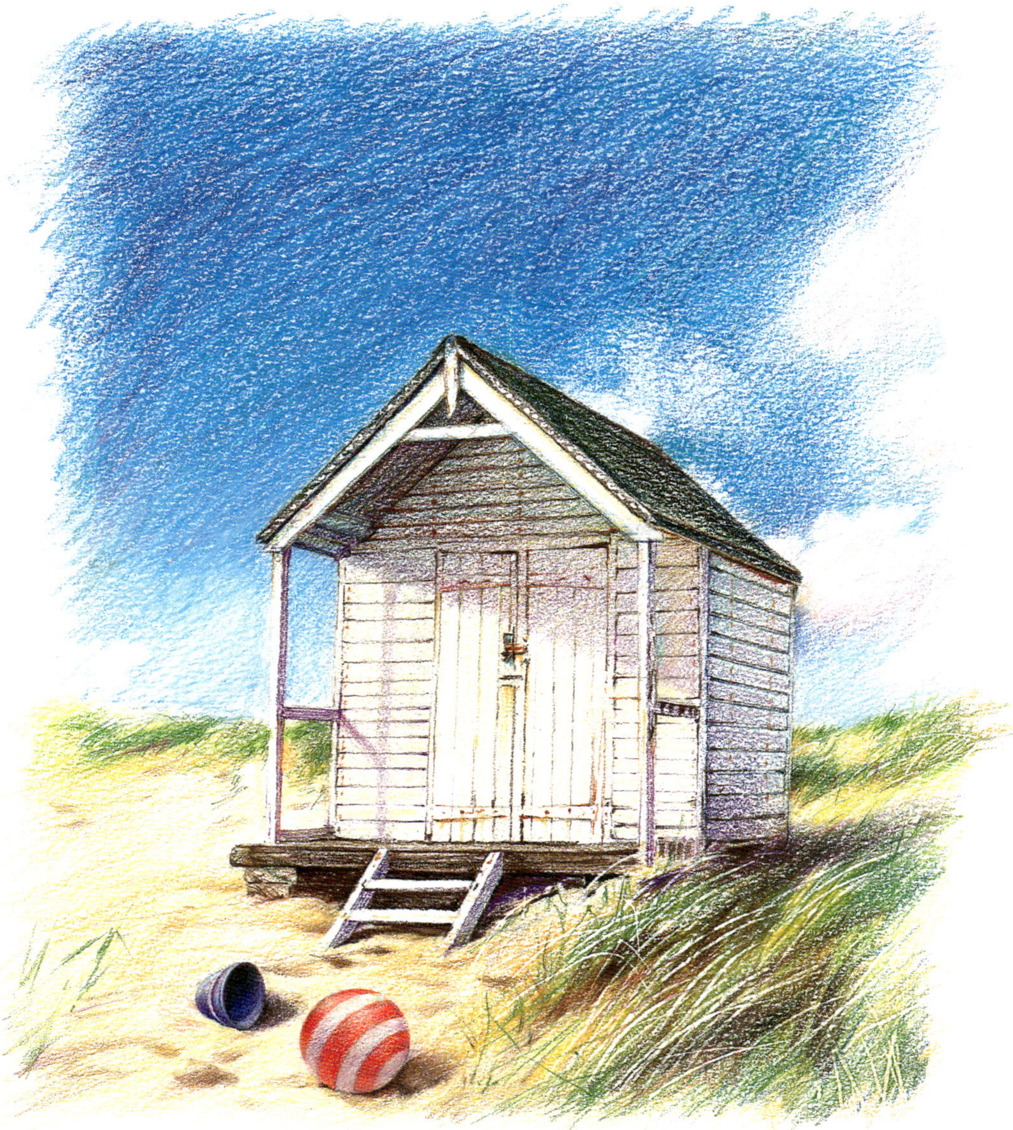

In this composition we see the perspective very clearly, the lines made by the boards on the side
of the beach hut converging towards the distant vanishing point.

To draw circular elements in perspective, whether in landscape or still life, it is useful to construct the ellipse (a circle in perspective) within a square (**fig.4**).

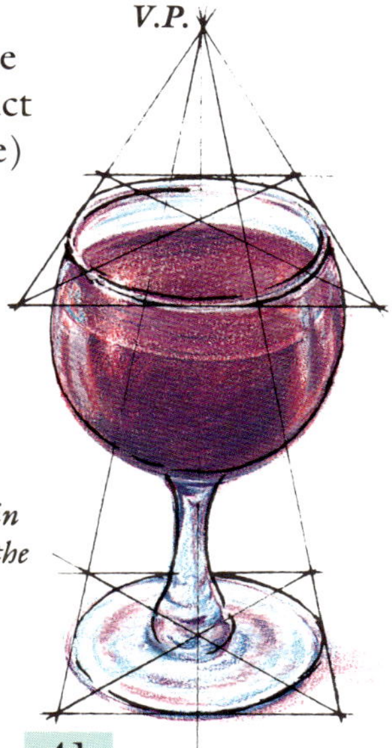

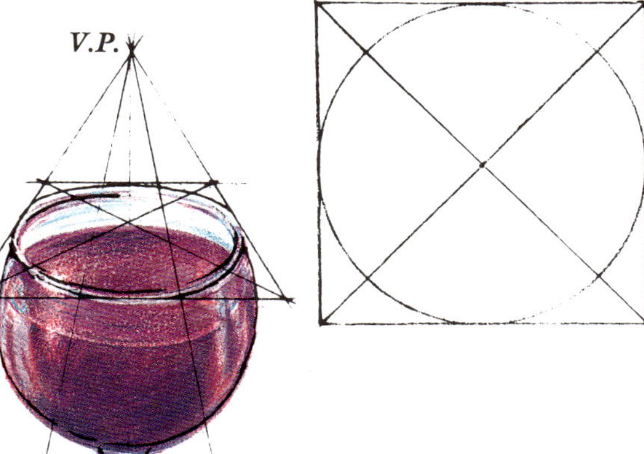

You may find it helpful to lightly pencil in perspective lines as with this study where the ellipses have been constructed within imagined squares.

Fig. 4

41

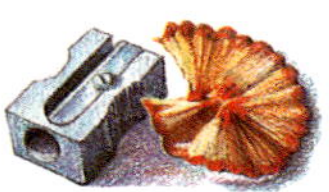

PORTRAITS & FIGURES

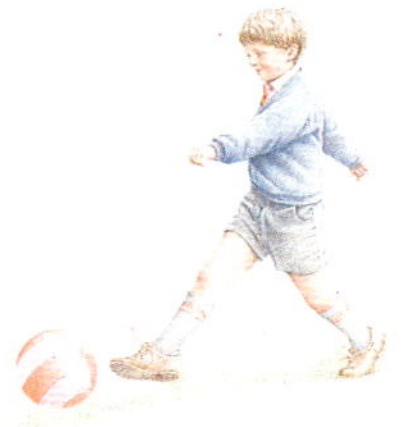

FOR MANY PEOPLE, THE ABILITY to portray another person successfully in a picture is considered the ultimate act of artistic creation. Be that as it may, but it is true to say that the study of other people is a fascinating and enduring subject.

To produce a successful portrait requires a knowledge and understanding of the subject reaching beyond the physical qualities. It is necessary to sense the moods, mannerisms and expressions of your sitter. As with landscape, it is important to steep yourself in your subject and to take in all the information you can.

Once you have gained an affinity with the subject – and only then – can you begin to plan your approach. Many preliminary sketches and photographs will assist you on your compositional choice. It is essential that every element is expressive of the person you are portraying. A portrait cannot work without these qualities, no matter how technically accomplished it is.

Right *A real up beat note of summer is captured in this portrait. The careful attention to the skin tones and bright sparkle of the eyes produce an image of health and vitality.*
Far Right *This group study is full of mystery, making the viewer wonder 'what are these two people doing and thinking?'.*
Using dark tinted paper helped me to create the sensation of strong sunlight streaming over the backs of the figures.

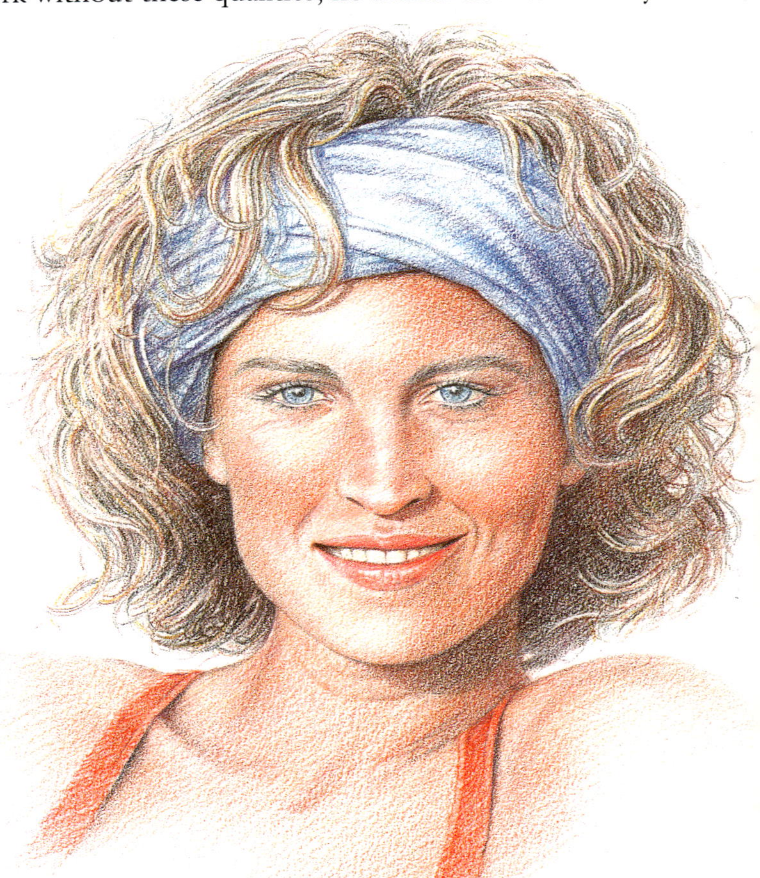

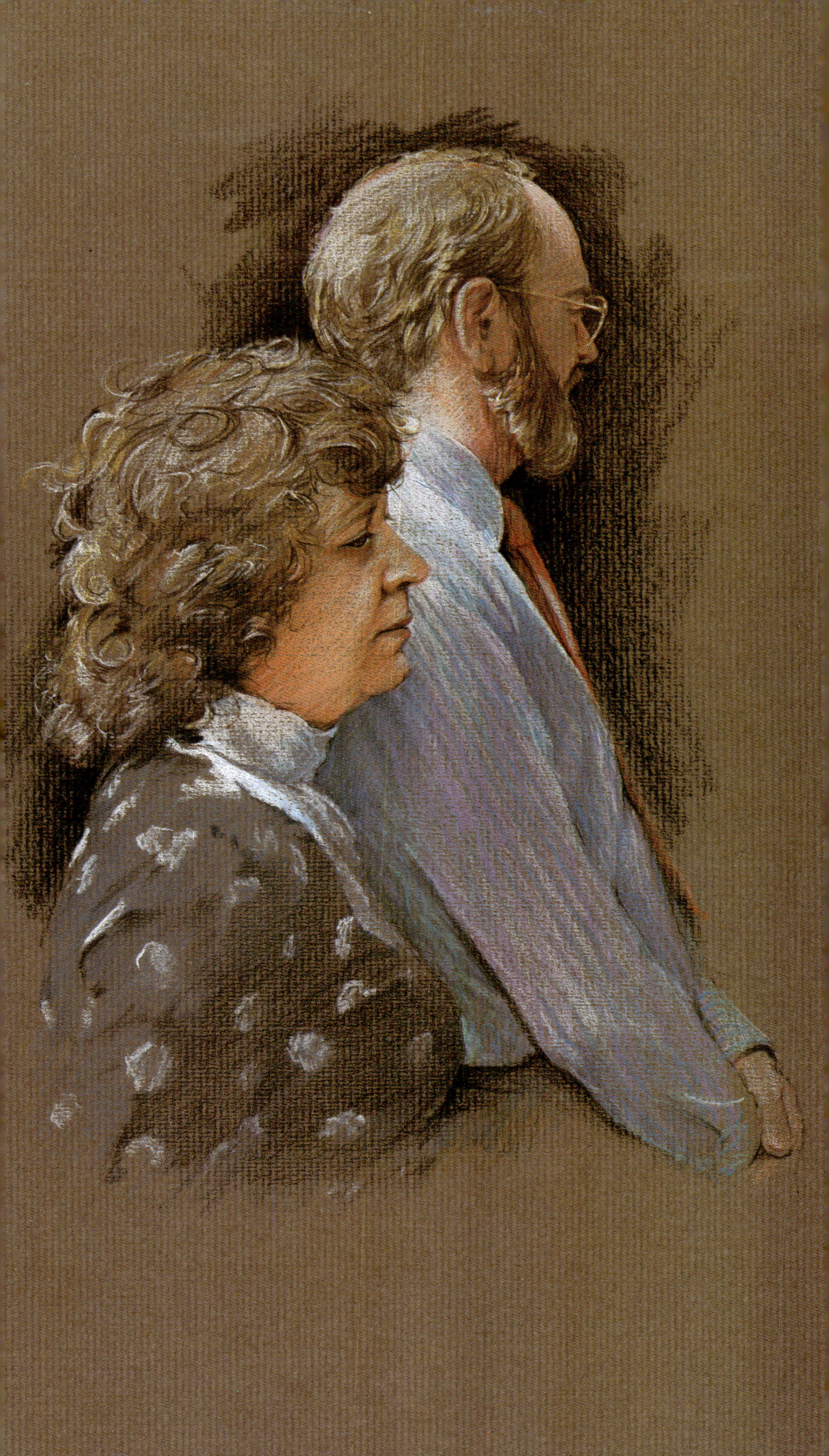

SALLY'S MOUSE

This portrait of my daughter captures her personality perfectly. The idea of the mouse was hers and seeing that it relaxed her to be holding it I went along with it. It also demonstrates her fun loving nature and passion for animals, making the picture quite a comprehensive portrayal of this young person. As you will see, I have used predominantly warm hues to enhance the joyous upbeat note of this portrait.

This step-by-step shows you the technical process: the rest is up to you!

Step 1: Using only burnt ochre I laid in the foundations of the face, concentrating on the eyes, mouth, hair and most obvious shadows.

Step 2: Before going any further I put in the fine highlights in the hair, using impressed line (described on page 14). After consolidating the shadows further, I applied a light layer of yellow ochre over the whole head, except for the highlights, giving the face a warm glow. Raw and burnt umber was used to define the structure and waves of the hair, the fine impressed lines showing up as thin strands of hair. Vermillion was then applied lightly to the cheeks, nose and lips, giving a luminous fresh quality to the skin. The hairband adds a colourful note to this portrait.

Step 3: Having established an overall tone and hue to the face I then deepened the shadows with burnt umber and vermillion under the chin and nose. The lighter skin tones were obtained using a soft coat of pale peach and the reflected light under the chin suggested with yellow ochre. A blue tint was put into the eyes and the pupils where darkened using indigo giving the eyes sparkle.

1

2

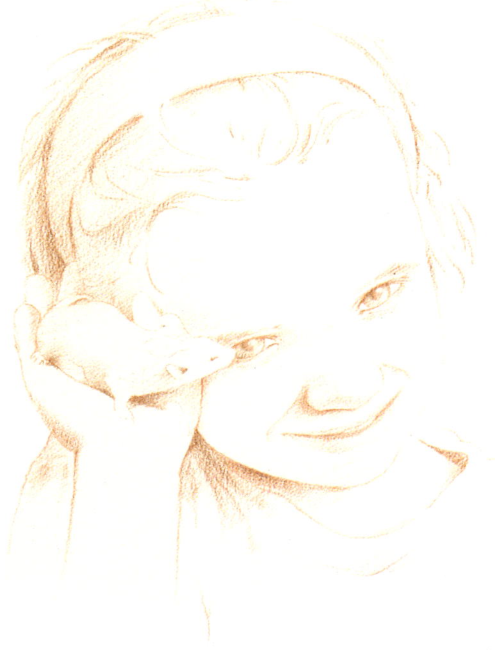

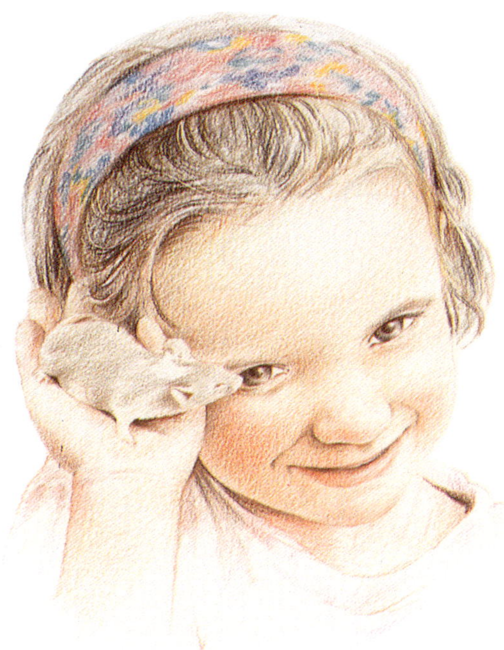

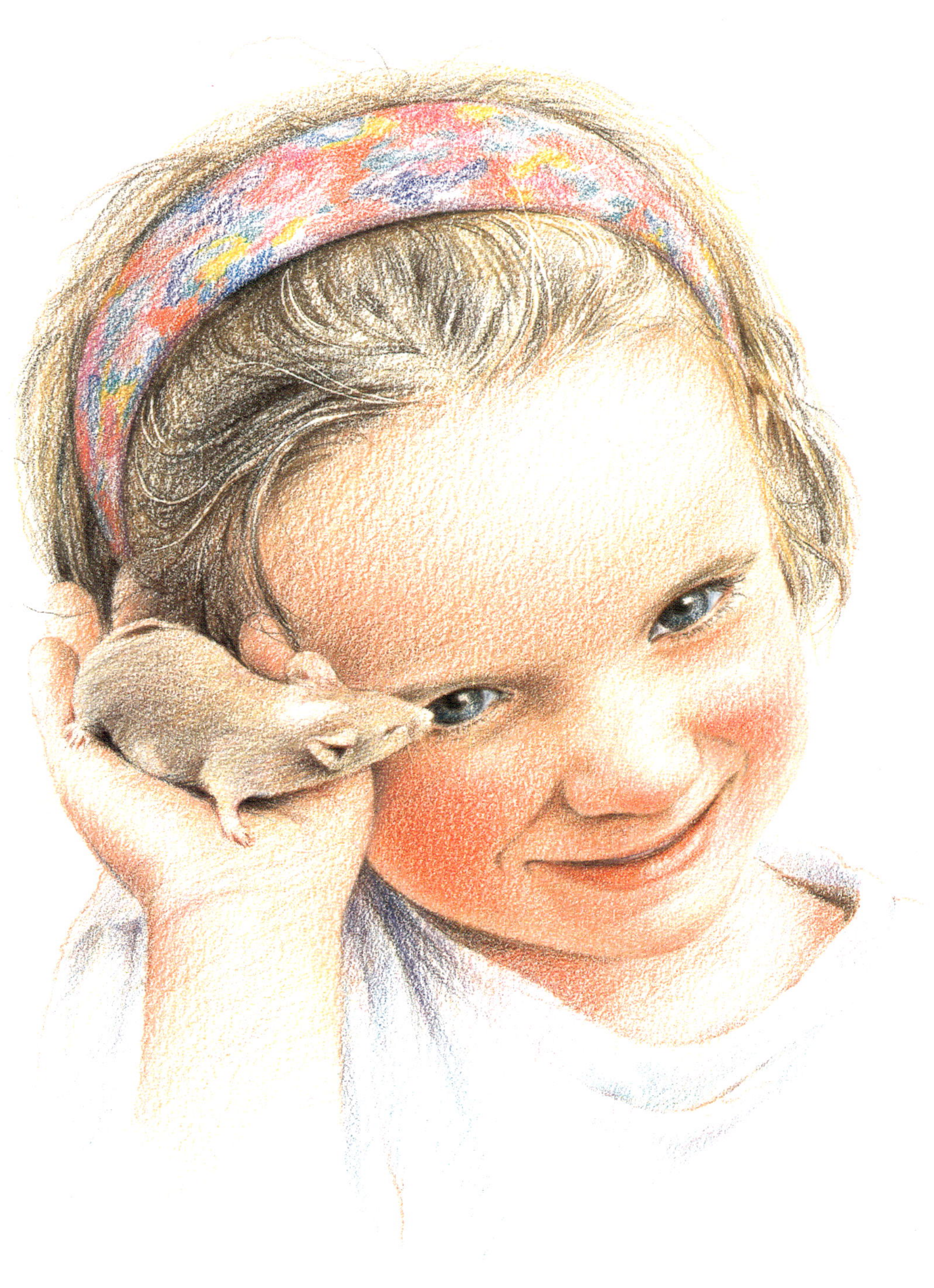

The final image is one of a young person with a warm character and a slightly mischievous glint in her eye.

At the beginning of the book, I mentioned the need to find a way of portraying the very essence of a subject for a drawing to have life and vitality. This is especially relevant with portrait and figure work. One of the best ways to achieve this is to capture your subject in their own environment, looking relaxed and at ease. Try to avoid the awful boardroom poses that are all too often given as examples of professional portraiture.

Drawing figures and figure groups where the identity of the subject is not known can be quite fascinating. Handled correctly, compositions of this kind can produce dynamic images that are full of movement and life.

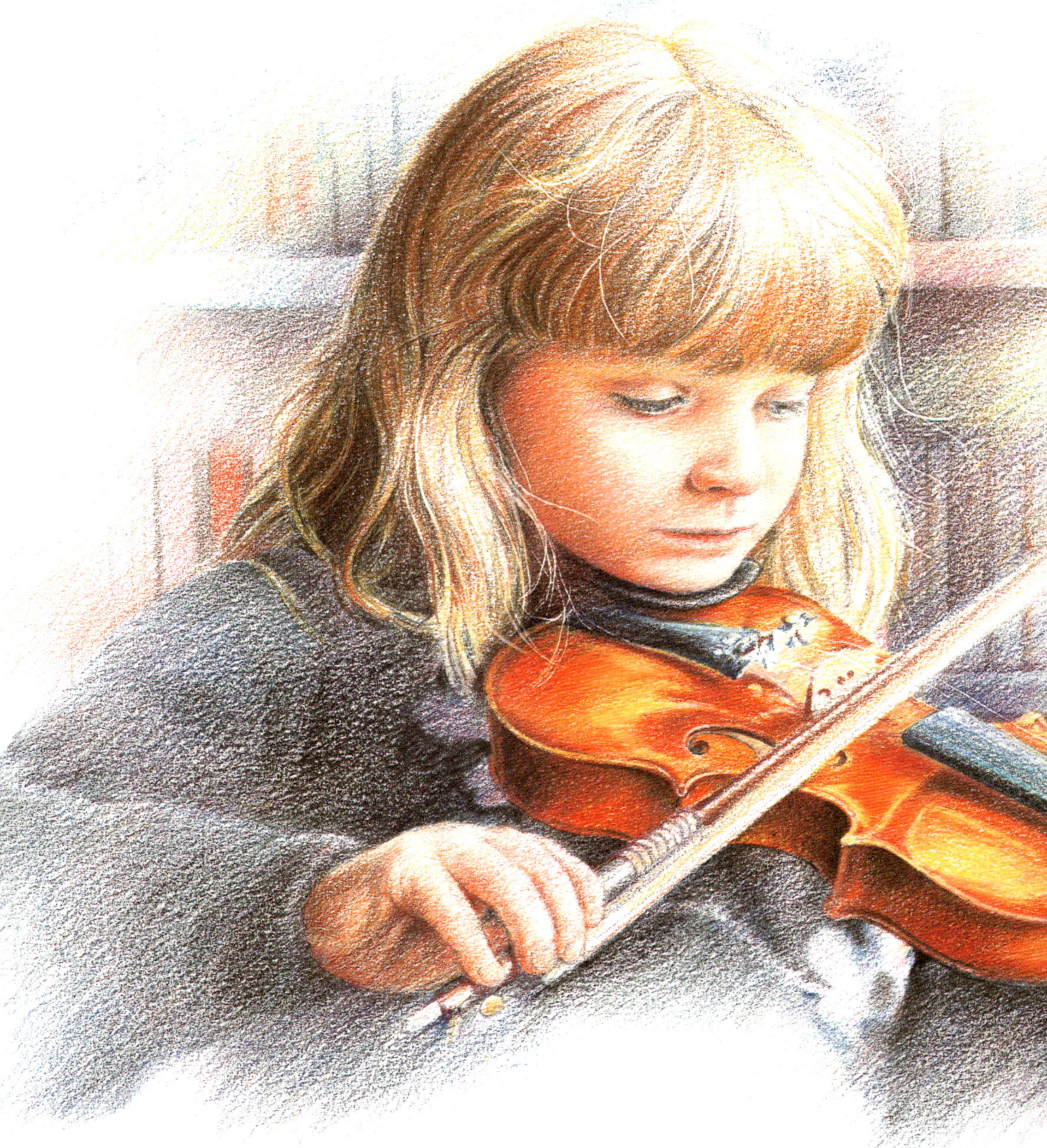

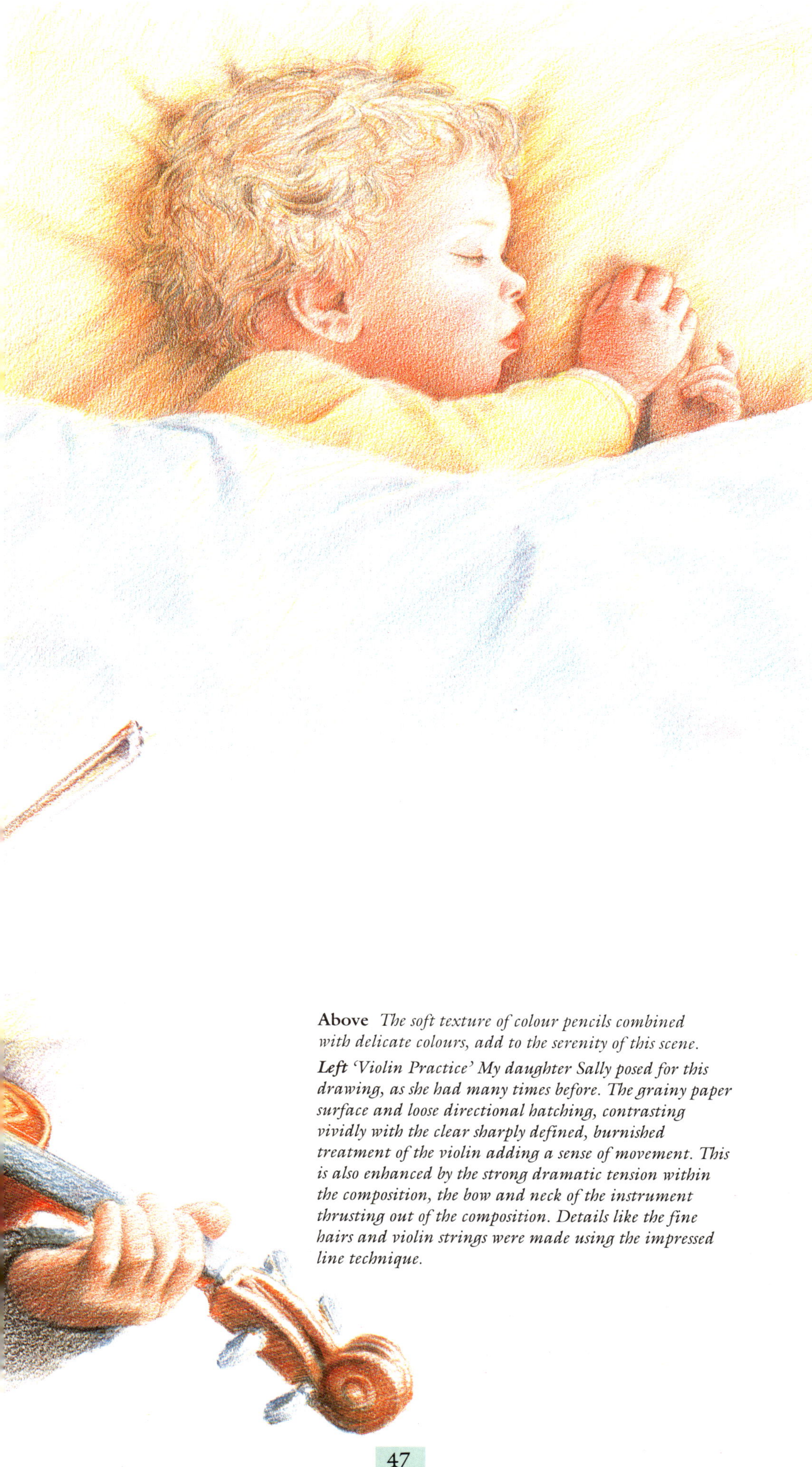

Above *The soft texture of colour pencils combined with delicate colours, add to the serenity of this scene.*

Left *'Violin Practice' My daughter Sally posed for this drawing, as she had many times before. The grainy paper surface and loose directional hatching, contrasting vividly with the clear sharply defined, burnished treatment of the violin adding a sense of movement. This is also enhanced by the strong dramatic tension within the composition, the bow and neck of the instrument thrusting out of the composition. Details like the fine hairs and violin strings were made using the impressed line technique.*

CONCLUSION

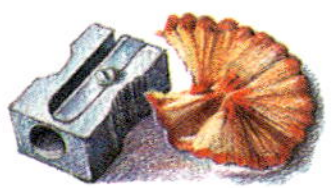

MY HOPE IS THAT, DURING the course of this book, it has become clear that colour pencils, far from being a limited medium associated only with childhood pencil boxes, are the tools of the artist. They are used as a starting point for many paintings and are capable of many uses, from rich highly finished work to sketches of depth and with great expression.

Most important is that you have discovered the pleasure of working with this clean and portable medium. Having tried out and practised the techniques and skills described, explore and challenge yourself further, constantly searching for new, challenging and exciting ways of applying coloured pencils.

Ultimately, the rules – once learned – are there to be broken. Don't be afraid to take risks and even to make the odd mistake. Only by doing this can you occasionally surprise yourself by coming up with something quite superlative. It is at these rare moments that you will feel the magic of creative work and the inspiration to reach that bit further and to try that bit harder – next time.

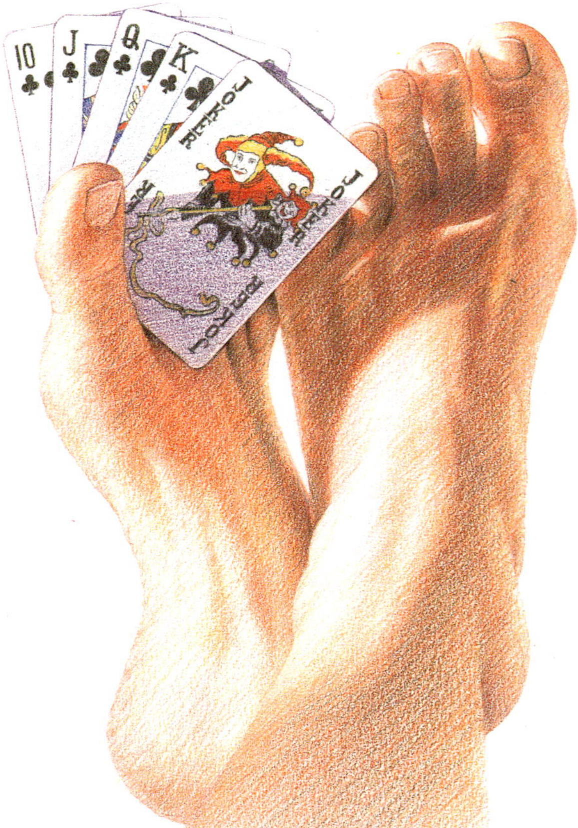